EVERYDAY Word

concordiafamily.org

CONCORDIA PUBLISHING HOUSE · SAINT LOUIS

Dedication

I thank God for my dear wife, Heather, who grew with me each day through my writing and our initial practicing of *Everyday Word: A Two-Year Bible Journal.*

I also thank the Lord for the support of this project that I have received from many dear fellow disciples of Jesus in The Lutheran Church—Missouri Synod, including members of the Board for National Missions, several district presidents, representatives from both seminaries and other schools of the Concordia University System, congregations, church workers, and committed laity.

Published by Concordia Publishing House
3558 S. Jefferson Ave., St. Louis, MO 63118-3968
1-800-325-3040 • cph.org

Copyright © 2025 Todd A. Biermann

All rights reserved. No part of this publication may be reproduced, stored in a retrieval system, or transmitted, in any form or by any means, electronic, mechanical, photocopying, recording, or otherwise, without the prior written permission of Concordia Publishing House.

Scripture quotations are from the ESV® Bible (The Holy Bible, English Standard Version®), copyright © 2001 by Crossway, a publishing ministry of Good News Publishers. Used by permission. All rights reserved.

Manufactured in the United States of America

1 2 3 4 5 6 7 8 9 10 34 33 32 31 30 29 28 27 26 25

CONTENTS

FOREWORD 8

INTRODUCTION 10

WEEK 1 (Genesis 1:1–12:9) 12

WEEK 2 (Genesis 12:10–22:24) 14

WEEK 3 (Genesis 23–35) 16

WEEK 4 (Genesis 36–44) 18

WEEK 5 (Genesis 45–50; Exodus 1–4) 20

WEEK 6 (Exodus 5–13) 22

WEEK 7 (Exodus 14–22) 24

WEEK 8 (Exodus 23–33) 26

WEEK 9 (Exodus 34–40; Leviticus 1–3) 28

WEEK 10 (Leviticus 4–19) 30

WEEK 11 (Leviticus 20–27; Numbers 1–8) 32

WEEK 12 (Numbers 9–21) 34

WEEK 13 (Numbers 22–36) 36

WEEK 14 (Deuteronomy 1–6) 38

WEEK 15 (Deuteronomy 7–15) 40

WEEK 16 (Deuteronomy 16–26) 42

WEEK 17 (Deuteronomy 27–32) 44

WEEK 18 (Deuteronomy 33–34; Joshua 1–7) 46

WEEK 19 (Joshua 8–19) 48

WEEK 20 (Joshua 20–24; Judges 1–2) 50

WEEK 21 (Judges 3–16) 52

WEEK 22 (Judges 17–21; Ruth 1–4; 1 Samuel 1) 54

WEEK 23 (1 Samuel 2–8) 56

WEEK 24 (1 Samuel 9–15) 58

WEEK 25 (1 Samuel 16–23) 60

WEEK 26 (1 Samuel 24–31) 62

WEEK 27 (2 Samuel 1–10) 64

WEEK 28 (2 Samuel 11–22) 66

WEEK 29 (2 Samuel 23–24; 1 Kings 1–8) 68

WEEK 30 (1 Kings 9–18) 70

WEEK 31 (1 Kings 19–22; 2 Kings 1–5) 72

WEEK 32 (2 Kings 6–16) 74

WEEK 33 (2 Kings 17–25) 76

WEEK 34 (1 Chronicles 1–17) 78

WEEK 35 (1 Chronicles 18–29) 80

WEEK 36 (2 Chronicles 1–12) 82

WEEK 37 (2 Chronicles 13–24) 84

WEEK 38 (2 Chronicles 25–33) 86

WEEK 39 (2 Chronicles 34–36; Ezra 1–8) 88

WEEK 40 (Ezra 9–10; Nehemiah 1–10) 90

WEEK 41 (Nehemiah 11–13; Esther 1–10; Job 1) 92

WEEK 42 (Job 2–14) 94

WEEK 43 (Job 15–31) 96

WEEK 44 (Job 32–42; Psalms 1–11) 98

WEEK 45 (Psalms 12–47) 100

WEEK 46 (Psalms 48–82) 102

WEEK 47 (Psalms 83–118) 104

WEEK 48 (Psalms 119–150) 106

WEEK 49 (Proverbs 1–9) 108

WEEK 50 (Proverbs 10–21) 110

WEEK 51 (Proverbs 22–31; Ecclesiastes 1–2) 112

WEEK 52 (Ecclesiastes 3–12; Song of Solomon 1–3) 114

WEEK 53 (Song of Solomon 4–8; Isaiah 1–6) 116

WEEK 54 (Isaiah 7–25) 118

WEEK 55 (Isaiah 26–39) 120

WEEK 56 (Isaiah 40–52) 122

WEEK 57 (Isaiah 53–66; Jeremiah 1–2) 124

WEEK 58 (Jeremiah 3–14) 126

WEEK 59 (Jeremiah 15–28) 128

WEEK 60 (Jeremiah 29–40) 130

WEEK 61 (Jeremiah 41–52; Lamentations 1) 132

WEEK 62 (Lamentations 2–5; Ezekiel 1–9) 134

WEEK 63 (Ezekiel 10–21) 136

WEEK 64 (Ezekiel 22–34) 138

WEEK 65 (Ezekiel 35–46) 140

WEEK 66 (Ezekiel 47–48; Daniel 1–6) 142

WEEK 67 (Daniel 7–12; Hosea 1–6) 144

WEEK 68 (Hosea 7–14; Joel 1) 146

WEEK 69 (Joel 2–3; Amos 1–6) 148

WEEK 70 (Amos 7–9; Obadiah; Jonah 1–4) 150

WEEK 71 (Micah 1–7; Nahum 1–3) 152

WEEK 72 (Habakkuk 1–3; Zephaniah 1–3; Haggai 1–2; Zechariah 1–2) 154

WEEK 73 (Zechariah 3–8) 156

WEEK 74 (Zechariah 9–14; Malachi 1–4) 158

WEEK 75 (Matthew 1–13) 160

WEEK 76 (Matthew 14–25) 162

WEEK 77 (Matthew 26–28; Mark 1–8) 164

WEEK 78 (Mark 9–15) 166

WEEK 79 (Mark 16; Luke 1–8) 168

WEEK 80 (Luke 9–16) 170

WEEK 81 (Luke 17–24; John 1–3) 172
WEEK 82 (John 4–14) 174
WEEK 83 (John 15–21; Acts 1–2) 176
WEEK 84 (Acts 3–12) 178
WEEK 85 (Acts 13–23) 180
WEEK 86 (Acts 24–28; Romans 1–6) 182
WEEK 87 (Romans 7–16) 184
WEEK 88 (1 Corinthians 1–10) 186
WEEK 89 (1 Corinthians 11–16; 2 Corinthians 1–4) 188
WEEK 90 (2 Corinthians 5–13; Galatians 1–2) 190
WEEK 91 (Galatians 3–6; Ephesians 1–3) 192
WEEK 92 (Ephesians 4–6; Philippians 1–4) 194
WEEK 93 (Colossians 1–4; 1 Thessalonians 1–3) 196
WEEK 94 (1 Thessalonians 4–5; 2 Thessalonians 1–3; 1 Timothy 1–2) 198
WEEK 95 (1 Timothy 3–6; 2 Timothy 1–2) 200
WEEK 96 (2 Timothy 3–4; Titus 1–3; Philemon; Hebrews 1) 202
WEEK 97 (Hebrews 2–7) 204
WEEK 98 (Hebrews 8–12) 206
WEEK 99 (Hebrews 13; James 1–5) 208
WEEK 100 (1 Peter 1–5; 2 Peter 1–3) 210
WEEK 101 (1 John 1–5; 2 John) 212
WEEK 102 (3 John; Jude; Revelation 1–5) 214
WEEK 103 (Revelation 6–13) 216
WEEK 104 (Revelation 14–19) 218
WEEK 105 (Revelation 20–22) 220

Foreword

Reading through the entire Bible is a life-changing activity. My good friend Rev. Dr. Todd Biermann understands this. As a former parish pastor, he also knows that many Christians *desire* to read all of God's Word but have not been able to do so. During the COVID-19 pandemic, this seasoned pastor saw an opportunity to help his church members accomplish this goal. So, he prepared a two-year Bible reading guide that became *Everyday Word: A Two-Year Bible Journal*. Through his position as executive director of Concordia Center for the Family, a churchwide organization serving homes and congregations in family discipleship, he now hopes this work can help other congregations.

There are many Bible reading plans available in print and digital media. As helpful as these may be, none can take you from Genesis to Revelation if not consistently used. Dr. Biermann's guide hits the sweet spot of providing basic background to inform the assigned readings while also inviting you to record reflections and responses to God's Word. His purpose is to draw you into consuming all of Scripture over two years in a way that the Spirit of God may craft a faithful response in your daily life. The desire is to enhance your journey through God's Word as an individual disciple or with your family in daily devotions.

It is interesting to note that the very important parts of this book are the blank spaces that invite your notes and reflections. They say to you, "Write in this book!" Todd understands that God, in His Word, invites us into conversation with Him. We listen and respond. Writing down our thoughts helps us organize and synthesize them, as the Holy Spirit creates in us a response to His Word.

I very much appreciate Todd's two-year-plan approach. The first time my wife and I were able to read through all of Holy Scripture was by using a two-year guide with simple supporting material, like what he provides in this book. Recently, members of a men's Bible study I attend at our church were discussing their desire to read the entire Bible. They also settled on a two-year plan they believe will help hold one another accountable to accomplish their goal. This book would serve them very well.

Journeys require effort. We know that many common distractions returned after the COVID-19 pandemic. *Everyday Word: A Two-Year Bible Journal* is an invitation to put forth effort needed to walk with God by being in His Word daily. This work starts with the divine revelation of the prophets and apostles and continues with His Spirit working in your life as you read and respond. Whether you are embarking on the journey as an individual, with family, or as part of a group from church, Dr. Biermann's guide can provide a simple path forward to help you effectively realize the goal of reading the entire Bible and growing as a disciple of Jesus Christ through the process.

I thank my dear friend Rev. Dr. Todd Biermann for providing this resource.

In Christ,

Dr. W. Mart Thompson

Associate professor of practical theology, Concordia Seminary, St. Louis, Missouri

Introduction

Welcome to YOUR Bible reading journal!

What you have before you is the fruit of a journey I traveled during a very challenging time in my ministry, when COVID-19 was wreaking havoc on every part of life, including corporate worship by the Body of Christ. As senior pastor of a large LCMS congregation, I sought to keep my flock engaged in God's Word, connected with their church family, and closely bound to their immediate family unit, even as the pandemic sought to interrupt all these connections. The Lord led me to produce this guide as one means to achieve those ends. Using this guide, by God's grace, the Word of God kept my congregation and its families growing together in faith as vibrant disciples of Jesus, even through such a highly disruptive time. I firmly believe it will continue to be a blessing to all who use it in any place and time, as each of us daily faces the disruption and distress of a dying world.

This resource will serve as the framework for you to create your own commentary on the entire Bible. The weekly units correspond to the weekly readings noted in "A Two-Year Reading Plan" on pages lix–lxiii at the front of *The Lutheran Study Bible* (*TLSB*) from Concordia Publishing House (CPH). By reading a short segment of Scripture every day, excluding Sundays, you'll be able to read the entire Bible in just over two years (105 weeks).

Each weekly unit has six primary components. For maximum benefit, I suggest you read through each week's material at the start of the week, perhaps on Sunday, taking note of connections to watch for in the Bible readings or jotting down ideas for application. Then, as you read or listen to the Bible texts each day, refer to this guide and use it to record your insights. The six components each week are as follows:

HISTORICAL CONTEXT—a brief introduction to the time, people, and places corresponding to the readings for the week

LAW AND GOSPEL THEMES—a brief consideration of key theological points that stand out in the week's readings, helping you recognize the destructive power of sin but the even greater restorative power of God's grace in Christ that permeates all of Scripture

LIFE APPLICATION STARTERS—questions to help you apply the readings and their teachings to your daily life as an individual, as part of a family, as part of a Christian congregation, and as a witness for Jesus Christ to the world. If you don't know how to answer any of the questions, turn to a fellow disciple or pastor for input. Asking questions is essential to growing as a disciple.

PRAYER STARTERS—several simple thoughts that prompt you to speak to the Lord in prayer about the themes presented in the readings, honoring, confessing, pleading, rejoicing, thanking, and praising our God, who desires to hear from you continually

WEEKLY MEMORY VERSES—special passages from the readings that week that are worthy of being committed to memory for lifelong benefit

DAILY READINGS AND NOTES—the list of readings for each day of the week, accompanied by writing space and prompts to promote personal meditation on the insights you will surely gain through this journey under the guidance of the Holy Spirit

Ideally, you will use this resource again and again for as long as you live. Once you complete the two-year journal, you can return to the start and do it all again, watching for the new discoveries the Lord will give you. Your recorded thoughts will expand year after year, making this your personal commentary on all of Scripture. Your faith will surely grow as you daily read, mark, learn, and inwardly digest the precious Word of God. Your growth will be enhanced as you turn to a fellow disciple or pastor to help answer your questions as they arise from your reading. Asking questions is essential to growing as a disciple.

I'm especially grateful for the partnership this book represents between CPH and the LCMS Recognized Service Organization of which I serve as executive director, Concordia Center for the Family (CCF, concordiafamily.org). CPH supports the mission of Concordia Center for the Family: uniting homes and congregations in making lifelong disciples of Jesus. The growth we receive as disciples of Jesus through weekly public gatherings with the Body of Christ will be enhanced and ingrained through continued study of the Word each day in the home. This growth at home is especially powerful when families or close friends gather in person to receive and discuss the Word of the Lord. For instance, family members can listen together to the Bible read out loud and then discuss based on the guides in this book. Those who live alone can read the Bible passages for the week on their own and then gather for discussion sparked by this guide. This resource represents a united effort between CPH and CCF to facilitate such vibrant, lifelong growth.

May the Lord grant you abundant blessings as you embark on your own Bible reading journey. I pray it will be the start of a deeper dive into the joyous life that is yours as a daily disciple of Jesus Christ, our Savior.

Rev. Dr. Todd A. Biermann

HISTORICAL CONTEXT

The readings this week include foundational events of history—the creation, the fall, the flood, and the tower of Babel. These are some of the most important chapters of the Bible, and you may want to take extra time to read through them. The first five books of the Bible, called the Pentateuch, were written by the prophet Moses from approximately 1446–1406 BC.

LAW AND GOSPEL THEMES

The Lord perfectly created this world and all relationships. Marriage between one man and one woman for life is foundational. The fall into sin brought death to man and all of creation. The only hope for salvation is in the promised Messiah (see Genesis 3:15). Men continued to reject the Lord until He caused the worldwide flood. Noah and his family were spared by faith in the Lord's promises. Men again rejected the Lord and trusted in their power, so He confused their language and scattered them at Babel. Peace and unity come only through faith in the Messiah, Jesus.

WEEKLY MEMORY VERSE

Genesis 2:24, "Therefore a man shall leave his father and his mother and hold fast to his wife, and they shall become one flesh."

LIFE APPLICATION STARTERS

What temptations most threaten your walk with the Lord? How have you fallen from Him in your life? Today? Adam and Eve were to support each other against temptation. Whom do you rely on for support? The flood and preparation for it tested Noah for a long time. What long-term trials test your faith? How? How did Noah endure? How do you? How are you, like the sinners of Babel, trusting in your own might? How is the curse of Babel still dividing mankind today? How can we (actually, the Lord) overcome this division?

PRAYER STARTERS

Pray for awareness of what tempts you to fall, for trust in the Messiah and all the Lord's promises, for fellow Christians who will walk with you in mutual accountability and support, and for the strength of Christian families and society as designed by the Lord.

DAILY READINGS AND NOTES

MONDAY	TUESDAY	WEDNESDAY
Genesis 1–2	Genesis 3	Genesis 4:1–6:8

THURSDAY	FRIDAY	SATURDAY
Genesis 6:9–8:22	Genesis 9–10	Genesis 11:1–12:9

NEW INSIGHTS

FURTHER QUESTIONS

PERSONAL PRAYERS

HISTORICAL CONTEXT

We focus this entire week on Abram, later called Abraham, the Lord's chosen ancestor of the Messiah, Jesus. In a period from around 2091–2046 BC, Abraham moved from Ur of the Chaldeans to Egypt for a time. Then he ended up in Canaan, the Promised Land, later known as Israel. The first five books of the Bible, called the Pentateuch, were written by the prophet Moses from approximately 1446–1406 BC.

LAW AND GOSPEL THEMES

Men continued to reject the Lord, but He graciously chose and preserved a faithful line from Adam to Noah to Abram. Abram, whose name the Lord changed to Abraham, acted in fear and doubt, but the Lord forgave and blessed him . . . many times (look for this pattern). The Lord mercifully answered Abraham's faith-filled prayer for Sodom, but judgment must fall on the impenitent. The Lord always keeps His covenant promises, regularly sealed by the shedding of lifeblood—a prime example, a substitute ram for Abraham's sacrifice in the place of Isaac, pointing clearly to Jesus as our substitute on the cross.

WEEKLY MEMORY VERSE

Genesis 15:6, "And [Abram] believed the LORD, and He counted it to him as righteousness."

LIFE APPLICATION STARTERS

Are you willing to GO when and where the Lord calls you? How has doubt kept you from following God's call? How has God worked good from evil in you and the world, sometimes in ways that seem miraculous? How does (and must) sacrificial blood still impact our lives today? What reasons and power sources do you have to trust the Lord and His ways? What comfort do you gain as you ponder the life of Abraham? What help and hope is there for your imperfect family?

PRAYER STARTERS

Pray for ears to hear and courage to go when and where the Lord leads; in thanksgiving for the Lord's mercy and grace in your life; for wisdom and courage to intercede and care for a sinful world; and for faithful reliance on Jesus' blood, still shed for us today.

DAILY READINGS AND NOTES

MONDAY	TUESDAY	WEDNESDAY
Genesis 12:10–13:18	Genesis 14–15	Genesis 16–17

THURSDAY	FRIDAY	SATURDAY
Genesis 18–19	Genesis 20–21	Genesis 22

NEW INSIGHTS

FURTHER QUESTIONS

PERSONAL PRAYERS

HISTORICAL CONTEXT

We conclude the story of Abraham with events that occurred from 2030–1991 BC, and we move on to the accounts of his son Isaac and twin grandsons Jacob and Esau, up to an estimated 1900 BC. The first five books of the Bible, called the Pentateuch, were written by the prophet Moses from approximately 1446–1406 BC.

LAW AND GOSPEL THEMES

Abraham showed his faith in the Lord's sure promises as he bought a plot of ground in the Promised Land to bury Sarah. The Lord clearly provided Rebekah as a wife for Isaac and blessed their marriage, especially with twin sons Jacob and Esau. Jacob was deceitful, and Esau was disrespectful and hateful. By grace, the Lord richly blessed Jacob even though he was undeserving. Despite displacement, betrayal, and fear for his life, Jacob was blessed with wives, wealth, and twelve sons. The Lord renamed Jacob *Israel*, which means "He strives with God," and his twelve sons became heads of the twelve chosen tribes of Israel.

WEEKLY MEMORY VERSE

Genesis 26:4, "I will multiply your offspring as the stars of heaven. . . . And in your offspring all the nations of the earth shall be blessed."

LIFE APPLICATION STARTERS

How does your faith in God's promises impact your decisions? When have you, like Isaac, Esau, Jacob, and his sons, acted in sin to get what you want when you want it? How have you, like each of these, been the recipient of mercy and grace from the Lord in spite of your sin? How has your example been misleading to your offspring? What are the most important things you can leave to your offspring?

PRAYER STARTERS

Pray for trust in the Lord's timing, mercy, and grace; for resistance against sin and the desire to do things your way; for wisdom in faithfully raising up the next generation to follow the Lord; and in thanksgiving for Jesus, who adopts you as a child of Abraham.

DAILY READINGS AND NOTES

MONDAY	TUESDAY	WEDNESDAY
Genesis 23–24	Genesis 25–26	Genesis 27–28

THURSDAY	FRIDAY	SATURDAY
Genesis 29–30	Genesis 31–33	Genesis 34–35

NEW INSIGHTS

FURTHER QUESTIONS

PERSONAL PRAYERS

HISTORICAL CONTEXT

After a brief account of Esau's descendants, we move on to the important account of Jacob's eleventh son, Joseph, and his family conflict, his slavery and imprisonment in Egypt, and his rise to power over Egypt. These events took place between an estimated 1900–1876 BC. The first five books of the Bible, called the Pentateuch, were written by the prophet Moses from approximately 1446–1406 BC.

LAW AND GOSPEL THEMES

Joseph was graciously chosen by the Lord as the instrument to preserve His chosen people, Israel. Joseph succumbed to pride, and his brothers to envy. Sexual sin had a destructive role as well. The Lord gave miraculous power to Joseph to interpret dreams and govern wisely. Joseph's brothers were plagued by their past sins and feared the expected retribution. Israel clung to its own control but finally succumbed to the Lord's incredible plan. The Lord continued to reveal the most incredible plan of deliverance, which later came through Israel's greatest descendant, Jesus.

WEEKLY MEMORY VERSE

Genesis 41:39, "Then Pharaoh said to Joseph, 'Since God has shown you all this, there is none so discerning and wise as you are.'"

LIFE APPLICATION STARTERS

How has the Lord used you for good in a way you did not expect? How has pride tainted the good He has done through you? What regrets and fears keep you from moving ahead? Whom do you most closely relate to in the readings this week? What warnings and comfort do these readings provide for you and your family? Where do you see Jesus in the story of Joseph?

PRAYER STARTERS

Pray in thanks for the Lord graciously using you for good, for humility as you are used by the Lord, for mercy and grace toward those who harm and hate you, for patience as the Lord is slow to reveal His perfect plans, and in thanksgiving that we have seen the fulfillment of the Lord's salvation plan in Jesus.

DAILY READINGS AND NOTES

MONDAY	TUESDAY	WEDNESDAY
Genesis 36–37	Genesis 38–39	Genesis 40

THURSDAY	FRIDAY	SATURDAY
Genesis 41:1–40	Genesis 41:41–57	Genesis 42–44

NEW INSIGHTS

FURTHER QUESTIONS

PERSONAL PRAYERS

HISTORICAL CONTEXT

Genesis concludes with Jacob and his family moving to Egypt, Joseph's great deeds, and then his subsequent death (approximately 1806 BC). Exodus starts about three hundred years later with the oppression of the Israelites, God's chosen deliverer, Moses, and the account of the exodus in approximately 1446 BC. The first five books of the Bible, called the Pentateuch, were written by the prophet Moses from approximately 1446–1406 BC.

LAW AND GOSPEL THEMES

Joseph died in Egypt but had sure faith God would guide the Israelites back to the Promised Land (see Genesis 50:24). Famine and death in Egypt reflected the curse of sin on all creation, yet God provided care through His chosen instrument Joseph, who is a "type" of the greatest deliverer to come from Israel, Jesus. (A type is a person, place, or event that foreshadows an aspect of Jesus fulfilling God's plan of salvation.) Israel's slavery reflects that of all mankind under sin. Moses foolishly sought to deliver his people by his own power and had to flee in guilt and shame. God graciously forgave Moses and sent him back to deliver Israel from slavery—another type of Jesus.

WEEKLY MEMORY VERSE

Exodus 3:14, "God said to Moses, 'I AM WHO I AM.' And He said, 'Say this to the people of Israel: "I AM has sent me to you."'"

LIFE APPLICATION STARTERS

What plans do you have in place for your death that show your faith in Jesus and the resurrection? What signs of sin's destructive power do you see in all of creation? How does God continue to deliver from this power of sin? In what ways are you a slave? In what ways have you rejected God and caused more trouble by trying to save yourself from your slavery? How does God continue to graciously deliver you?

PRAYER STARTERS

Pray for faith in God's promises that give hope beyond the grave; for the preservation of all creation from sin's destructive power; in repentance for trying to be your own savior; for humility to serve as God's instrument to save others; and for complete trust in THE Savior, Jesus.

DAILY READINGS AND NOTES

MONDAY	TUESDAY	WEDNESDAY
Genesis 45–46	Genesis 47–48	Genesis 49–50
THURSDAY	**FRIDAY**	**SATURDAY**
Exodus 1	Exodus 2	Exodus 3–4

NEW INSIGHTS

FURTHER QUESTIONS

PERSONAL PRAYERS

HISTORICAL CONTEXT

Moses returned to Egypt as God's chosen deliverer. He and his brother, Aaron, delivered God's judgment to Pharaoh, which led to Israel's flight from Egypt and took them to the shore of the Red Sea around 1446 BC. The first five books of the Bible, called the Pentateuch, were written by the prophet Moses from approximately 1446–1406 BC.

LAW AND GOSPEL THEMES

God's means of deliverance for Israel seemed terrible at first, as their oppression only increased. God patiently provided Aaron to help his fearful brother, Moses. The ten plagues against Egypt showed God's sovereign power over all false gods. Death is the payment for sin, in this case, of the firstborn. The blood of a substitutionary sacrifice, a spotless lamb, protected the firstborn sons of the Israelites. The Lord passed over the homes of those who had marked their doors with the blood of a sacrificial lamb. The Passover is to be remembered through all generations. Jesus is our sacrificial substitute, so death will pass over us. God gave Israel a safe exodus, a way out, from slavery.

WEEKLY MEMORY VERSE

Exodus 12:13, "The blood shall be a sign for you, on the houses where you are. And when I see the blood, I will pass over you, and no plague will befall you to destroy you, when I strike the land of Egypt."

LIFE APPLICATION STARTERS

How has God's good plan for your life seemed unbearable at first? Whom has God given you to follow His way? How has He helped you follow His way? How do the ten plagues against Egypt convict you of idol worship? How can and should we observe the Passover today? What exodus awaits every Christian? How does this comfort you?

PRAYER STARTERS

Pray for perseverance when God's plan for you seems impossible; in thanksgiving for the helpers God provides, and to be a helper to others; for recognition to reject false gods; for forgiveness and strength in the Lord's Supper; and for confidence in the hope of your resurrection to life in heaven.

DAILY READINGS AND NOTES

MONDAY	TUESDAY	WEDNESDAY
Exodus 5–6	Exodus 7	Exodus 8–9

THURSDAY	FRIDAY	SATURDAY
Exodus 10	Exodus 11–12	Exodus 13

NEW INSIGHTS

FURTHER QUESTIONS

PERSONAL PRAYERS

HISTORICAL CONTEXT

Around 1446 BC, Moses and the nation of Israel continued their flight from Pharaoh and slavery in Egypt, passing through the Red Sea and coming to Mount Sinai. The first five books of the Bible, called the Pentateuch, were written by the prophet Moses from approximately 1446–1406 BC.

LAW AND GOSPEL THEMES

The Israelites cried out in despair as the sea stood before them with Pharaoh's army close behind. God delivered His chosen people through the sea and destroyed the pursuing army. This is a type of our deliverance from the destruction of hell through the waters of Baptism—God's work beyond our power. Praise is our fitting response. The Israelites quickly forgot God's care for them, worrying about food and water. God graciously provided what they need. Moses received wise counsel from his father-in-law, Jethro. At Sinai, the Lord renewed His covenant with Israel, and they responded with promised obedience. The Ten Commandments and further laws were given in love to Moses.

WEEKLY MEMORY VERSE

Exodus 20:3, "You shall have no other gods before Me."

LIFE APPLICATION STARTERS

What insurmountable obstacles fill you with fear and doubt in God's power to deliver? What comfort is yours through daily remembrance of your Baptism? How has God always provided for your needs of body and soul? How might you benefit from the advice of those nearest to you, particularly your family? Has God ever broken His covenant promises (see Exodus 19)? How are the Ten Commandments and other laws from the Lord good?

PRAYER STARTERS

Pray for trust in God in the face of great obstacles; for remembrance of your Baptism and its daily power; for trust in God for daily bread; for ears to hear wise advice from family and a mouth to speak God's wisdom; and in thanks for God's Commandments as you see their blessings.

DAILY READINGS AND NOTES

MONDAY	TUESDAY	WEDNESDAY
Exodus 14	Exodus 15	Exodus 16–17
THURSDAY	**FRIDAY**	**SATURDAY**
Exodus 18	Exodus 19–20	Exodus 21–22

NEW INSIGHTS

FURTHER QUESTIONS

PERSONAL PRAYERS

HISTORICAL CONTEXT

Moses met with the Lord on Mount Sinai around 1446 BC, following the deliverance of Israel from Egyptian slavery and prior to their wilderness wanderings. The first five books of the Bible, called the Pentateuch, were written by the prophet Moses from approximately 1446–1406 BC.

LAW AND GOSPEL THEMES

The Lord gave Moses many laws to warn of sin and to guide the Israelites toward His holy and blessed ways. Observance of the Sabbath and a physical place of worship were central. The Lord renewed His covenant promises with His people, including news about the land He had prepared for them. The Lord taught proper alignment of priorities through the wise stewardship of material and time. Keeping the Sabbath with time and action was an essential practice and habit for God's people—a matter of life and death. God's people were quick to turn to idol worship and the way of death. In love, the Lord punishes sinners and restores the penitent. Moses spoke with the Lord face to face as a friend.

WEEKLY MEMORY VERSE

Exodus 29:45, "I will dwell among the people of Israel and will be their God."

LIFE APPLICATION STARTERS

How do God's commands turn us from destruction and guide us to blessings? Why is weekly worship in a sacred space essential to our faith? How is the wise stewardship of our time and treasures important in keeping our priorities straight? What idols most tempt you to forget the Lord? Does the Lord punish us for our good? How can and should we talk with the Lord "face to face, as a man speaks to his friend" regularly (33:11)?

PRAYER STARTERS

Pray to remember and use the Lord's commands to know sin and return to Him; to cling to the hope of our promised land, heaven; to remain faithful in weekly worship in sacred time and space; to be a wise steward with the right priorities in all of life; to receive the Lord's discipline for good; and to daily talk to Jesus as a friend.

DAILY READINGS AND NOTES

MONDAY	TUESDAY	WEDNESDAY
Exodus 23–24	Exodus 25–27	Exodus 28–29
THURSDAY	**FRIDAY**	**SATURDAY**
Exodus 30–31	Exodus 32	Exodus 33

NEW INSIGHTS

FURTHER QUESTIONS

PERSONAL PRAYERS

HISTORICAL CONTEXT

God directed Moses to carve two new tablets of stone to replace the ones he had broken in anger. Then, God gave His Word in writing again. Exodus concludes with God directing the making and support of the tabernacle. Leviticus begins with the usage of the tabernacle and instructions for offerings. All these events took place in 1445 BC. The first five books of the Bible, called the Pentateuch, were written by the prophet Moses from approximately 1446–1406 BC.

LAW AND GOSPEL THEMES

Moses broke the first set of tablets containing God's Law, reflecting how the people had broken God's covenant with them. Yet God graciously renewed His covenant with them as He inscribed the tablets again. Israel was warned not to make any covenant with pagans. God prescribed regular "holy habits" for His people in the way of Sabbath observance and holy offerings. Details for the tabernacle and its furnishings showed God's concern for every aspect of Israel's worship life. Light and mercy reflect God's glorious love. Incense and offerings were to be given in response to God's mercy and grace.

WEEKLY MEMORY VERSE

Exodus 34:6, "The LORD the LORD, a God merciful and gracious, slow to anger, and abounding in steadfast love and faithfulness."

LIFE APPLICATION STARTERS

How has your sin led to brokenness and more work, even though it's forgiven? What does the giving of the Law to Moses teach us about all of Scripture? What wisdom for you today comes from Exodus 34:12? What habits do we practice in our church and home life today that reflect the tabernacle activities and furnishings? What does such detail teach about God's concern for our habits of worship?

PRAYER STARTERS

Pray to be forgiven for acting rashly and foolishly, for patience under the consequences of sin, to see God's mercy and grace in worship centered on His Word and Sacraments, to offer all you are and have in thankful service to God, and for good habits of regularly receiving and responding in worship.

DAILY READINGS AND NOTES

MONDAY	TUESDAY	WEDNESDAY
Exodus 34	Exodus 35–36	Exodus 37–38

THURSDAY	FRIDAY	SATURDAY
Exodus 39–40	Leviticus 1	Leviticus 2–3

NEW INSIGHTS

FURTHER QUESTIONS

PERSONAL PRAYERS

HISTORICAL CONTEXT

The Lord called Moses' brother, Aaron, and his sons as priests to serve in the newly constructed tabernacle. This established a life of holy worship for the Israelites. In 1445 BC, they were in the wilderness of Sinai after fleeing from Egypt. The first five books of the Bible, called the Pentateuch, were written by the prophet Moses from approximately 1446–1406 BC.

LAW AND GOSPEL THEMES

Sin corrupted the people of Israel . . . and corrupts ALL people. God is holy and demands His people to be holy—set apart from sin. Holiness is received by God's act of cleansing or redemption, ultimately through Jesus. The shedding of blood in animal sacrifice was powerful only because it is an antitype of Jesus and His shed blood, which purchased atonement for us. God expects our response to be a life of holiness, especially by those who serve Him as priests and teachers. No family is immune to sin, and all must daily flee to the Lord for gracious cleansing and holy guidance.

WEEKLY MEMORY VERSE

Leviticus 11:44, "For I am the LORD your God. Consecrate yourselves therefore, and be holy, for I am holy."

LIFE APPLICATION STARTERS

Why is holiness such a big deal with God? (Go back to creation in Genesis.) What does God require of you—in the place of animal sacrifices—to gain holiness? Priests and their practice are types of what in Christian life today? Why are the daily activities of eating, cleaning, sexual interaction, and child-rearing so important to God, both then and now? How can each of these be holy?

PRAYER STARTERS

Pray for open confession of your sin and lack of holiness; for faithful pastors and teachers to serve you with God's gifts and guide you to holiness; to see all parts of your daily life—food, chores, sex, education—as gifts from your holy God that are to be kept holy; and that you will always be a worthy example for others to follow, starting in your own home.

DAILY READINGS AND NOTES

MONDAY	TUESDAY	WEDNESDAY
Leviticus 4–6	Leviticus 7–9	Leviticus 10–11

THURSDAY	FRIDAY	SATURDAY
Leviticus 12–15	Leviticus 16–17	Leviticus 18–19

NEW INSIGHTS

FURTHER QUESTIONS

PERSONAL PRAYERS

HISTORICAL CONTEXT

In 1445 BC, Moses, Aaron, and the Israelites were in the wilderness of Sinai on their way from Mount Sinai to the Promised Land. The first five books of the Bible, called the Pentateuch, were written by the prophet Moses from approximately 1446–1406 BC.

LAW AND GOSPEL THEMES

God's call to holiness continued, especially among the priests. "I am the LORD" was a warning and a promise. Observance of sacred feasts and Sabbath time was a requirement and blessing, promising true rest and much more for body and soul. According to the censuses that were taken in Numbers 1 and 26 (hence its name "Numbers"), Israel had approximately 2.2 million people when they left Egypt. Incredibly, God graciously sustained this throng in the wilderness as they began their slow journey toward the Promised Land of Canaan. He comforted them with the blessing that was to be proclaimed to them by Aaron and his sons (see Numbers 6:22–27).

WEEKLY MEMORY VERSE

Numbers 6:24–26 (the Aaronic blessing), "The LORD bless you and keep you; the LORD make His face to shine upon you and be gracious to you; the LORD lift up His countenance upon you and give you peace."

LIFE APPLICATION STARTERS

How does the Sabbath apply to us today (see Leviticus 23:3)? How do you receive true rest from the Lord in "Sabbath time" on Sunday and throughout the week? How and why do the feasts of Israel prefigure our liturgical life? Why is holy convocation, the special gathering of God's people, important? Why is confession and forgiveness still part of our lives as God's people? How is God's name still placed upon us in rich blessing?

PRAYER STARTERS

Pray to properly fear the name of the Lord, to properly observe the liturgical calendar as a guide to holy living (receiving from and responding to God), to never neglect the convocation of the saints, that the wayward would return to the communal worship and blessings of the Lord, and to be a witness to those not yet numbered in the new Israel.

DAILY READINGS AND NOTES

MONDAY	TUESDAY	WEDNESDAY
Leviticus 20–22	Leviticus 23–25	Leviticus 26–27

THURSDAY	FRIDAY	SATURDAY
Numbers 1–3	Numbers 4–6	Numbers 7–8

NEW INSIGHTS

FURTHER QUESTIONS

PERSONAL PRAYERS

HISTORICAL CONTEXT

The Israelites moved from Mount Sinai to Kadesh to Moab in the region across the Jordan River to the east of Canaan, spanning 1445–1407 BC. The first five books of the Bible, called the Pentateuch, were written by the prophet Moses from approximately 1446–1406 BC.

LAW AND GOSPEL THEMES

The Passover was to be a key celebration in the life of Israel. God was incarnate, visible, in cloud and fire. Complaining and rebellion had plagued Israel from the start of their wanderings, and they suffered fire and destruction as a result. God's Spirit strengthened Moses and the seventy elders. God fed Israel with quail but punished the faithless. Jealousy and strife separated Moses from his siblings Miriam and Aaron. God honored Moses' plea for his people with pardon. Still, ten out of twelve spies did not trust the Lord, and the nation followed them to death during forty years of wandering. Jealousy again brought death to the greater family of Israel in Korah's rebellion. God showed favor to Aaron as his staff budded. Moses would suffer for using his action rather than relying on God's Word to bring forth water at Meribah. A fiery serpent is a type of Jesus.

WEEKLY MEMORY VERSE

Numbers 21:8, "And the LORD said to Moses, 'Make a fiery serpent and set it on a pole, and everyone who is bitten, when he sees it, shall live.'"

LIFE APPLICATION STARTERS

How does observance of the Passover still bless you? Where do you SEE God guiding you today? How has complaining and jealousy separated you from God and family with bitter consequences? Where is God leading you that requires bold faith? What will convince people to trust God? Do you lift your eyes to Jesus for delivery from death?

PRAYER STARTERS

Pray to rightly receive the Lord's Supper; to see God in His Word and Sacraments; for God to forgive your jealousy and complaints and heal your soul, family, church, and the world; to go where God leads with courage; and to witness of your Savior, Jesus, with God's mighty Word.

DAILY READINGS AND NOTES

MONDAY	TUESDAY	WEDNESDAY
Numbers 9–10	Numbers 11–12	Numbers 13–15

THURSDAY	FRIDAY	SATURDAY
Numbers 16–18	Numbers 19–20	Numbers 21

NEW INSIGHTS

FURTHER QUESTIONS

PERSONAL PRAYERS

HISTORICAL CONTEXT

In 1407 BC, the Israelites camped on and then settled in the plains of Moab, across the Jordan to the east of Canaan, as they awaited God's direction to enter the Promised Land. The first five books of the Bible, called the Pentateuch, were written by the prophet Moses from approximately 1446–1406 BC.

LAW AND GOSPEL THEMES

Those who seek to curse God's people against His will are in a losing battle. Sometimes a donkey is wiser than a prophet. Sin and idolatry were condemned in graphic terms as the Israelites followed their lusts and the gods of Moab. Phinehas lashed out violently for the Lord and received God's covenant of peace. God showed His care for women in providing for the daughters of Zelophehad. Joshua was set aside to take the place of Moses. Joshua's name clearly declared him to be a type of Jesus. Offerings gave God's people a way to thank and praise their Lord and Savior. Numbers 33 recounts Israel's journey with its sins and blessings.

WEEKLY MEMORY VERSE

Numbers 23:19, "God is not man, that He should lie, or a son of man, that He should change His mind. Has He said, and will He not do it? Or has He spoken, and will He not fulfill it?"

LIFE APPLICATION STARTERS

Have you ever found yourself in a losing battle with God? Even now? Wise up and be blessed. What temptations from the world try to draw you into lustful and idolatrous ways? When might it be fitting for God's people to act in righteous anger? How does God continue to show His care for women? How can names point eyes to Jesus? How can the giving of offerings be a blessing for US? Why is it important to regularly recount the history of God and His people?

PRAYER STARTERS

Pray to stop fighting against the will of God, for eyes and ears to see and hear God's direction that is consistent with His Word, to avoid the lure of the world, to know when to boldly rise against sin in God's power, that all people will be valued, and to remember and share the mighty deeds of God on our behalf.

DAILY READINGS AND NOTES

MONDAY	TUESDAY	WEDNESDAY
Numbers 22–25	Numbers 26–27	Numbers 28–30
THURSDAY	**FRIDAY**	**SATURDAY**
Numbers 31	Numbers 32–34	Numbers 35–36

NEW INSIGHTS

FURTHER QUESTIONS

PERSONAL PRAYERS

HISTORICAL CONTEXT

The Israelites remained encamped on the plains of Moab, across the Jordan, east of Canaan, in 1407 BC as they awaited God's direction to enter the Promised Land. The first five books of the Bible, called the Pentateuch, were written by the prophet Moses from approximately 1446–1406 BC.

LAW AND GOSPEL THEMES

Moses restated the history of God's deliverance from Egypt so the new generation wouldn't forget it. Thirty-eight years of wilderness wandering gave the Gentile nations an opportunity to repent before they were overtaken. The people and places described in Deuteronomy have present geography and archaeological support. Chapter 4 speaks of cities of refuge, which are types of Jesus, our Refuge. Chapter 5 restates God's covenant centered on the Ten Commandments, a blessing to those called to faith by His Word. Deuteronomy 6:4 is the *Shema* (Hear), an early creed of faith still used today. Deuteronomy 6:7, *Shanan* (Teach), directs parents to teach God's Word always. Deuteronomy 6:20 directs the catechetical practice of question and answer, later used by Luther in his Small Catechism.

WEEKLY MEMORY VERSE

Deuteronomy 6:6–7, "And these words that I command you today shall be on your heart. You shall teach them diligently to your children, and shall talk of them when you sit in your house, and when you walk by the way, and when you lie down, and when you rise."

LIFE APPLICATION STARTERS

Regularly recount the WHOLE history of God's gracious deliverance, noting real people and places, especially Jesus. How can God use you as He did Israel to lead more to repent and come to Him? How is Jesus your refuge? Know and review the Ten Commandments and the Apostles' Creed daily to grow in faith. Teach children God's Word through Q and A as you go along your daily way, answering, "What does this mean?"

PRAYER STARTERS

Pray in thanks to God for His history of deliverance from Adam, to Egypt, to Jesus, to today; for many to heed God's call through us and be led by the Spirit to repentance and faith in Jesus; in thanks for your refuge in Jesus; to always HEAR the Word of God and keep it; for the next generations to learn the Word of God and grow in faith through daily Q and A.

DAILY READINGS AND NOTES

MONDAY	TUESDAY	WEDNESDAY
Deuteronomy 1	Deuteronomy 2	Deuteronomy 3
THURSDAY	**FRIDAY**	**SATURDAY**
Deuteronomy 4	Deuteronomy 5	Deuteronomy 6

NEW INSIGHTS

FURTHER QUESTIONS

PERSONAL PRAYERS

HISTORICAL CONTEXT

The Israelites remained encamped on the plains of Moab, across the Jordan, east of Canaan, in 1407 BC as they awaited God's direction to enter the Promised Land. The first five books of the Bible, called the Pentateuch, were written by the prophet Moses from approximately 1446–1406 BC.

LAW AND GOSPEL THEMES

Deuteronomy 7:3 stresses not to intermarry with pagans, or they will lead us from faith to eternal destruction. Deuteronomy 8:3 reminds us we live not by bread alone but by the Word of God. Verse 5 speaks of God's discipline out of love. Chapter 9 makes clear that we are saved by grace through faith, pointing to Ephesians 2:5. Then we are called in 10:16 to circumcise our hearts, cutting away sinful selfishness so we can focus only on the Lord in faith. The second half of chapter 11 reminds us again of the importance of teaching God's Word and blessings to children as we go along the way every day, making it a godly habit. Chapter 12 makes clear that worship is not to be according to our feelings but God's way. Chapters 14–15 outline righteous ways to handle food, tithes, lending, and more.

WEEKLY MEMORY VERSE

Deuteronomy 8:3, "And He humbled you and let you hunger and fed you with manna . . . that He might make you know that man does not live by bread alone, but man lives by every word that comes from the mouth of the Lord."

LIFE APPLICATION STARTERS

How much should our faith influence who we marry? How regularly should we "feed" on God's Word? Are you an eager disciple of Jesus, even when it's tough? What place do good deeds have in your salvation? How is teaching God's ways to the young a regular habit for you? How does worship keep you focused on God, not on your own wants, ways, and feelings? Do you honor God with your food, wealth, and all things?

PRAYER STARTERS

Pray for faith in Jesus to guide all who seek a spouse; to hunger for God's Word always; to bear discipline from God for your good; that grace will save you and inspire your service; for the young to learn of Jesus from you in all you do and say; to worship in God's way, not your own; and to honor God with all you are and have.

DAILY READINGS AND NOTES

MONDAY	TUESDAY	WEDNESDAY
Deuteronomy 7	Deuteronomy 8	Deuteronomy 9–10

THURSDAY	FRIDAY	SATURDAY
Deuteronomy 11–12	Deuteronomy 13	Deuteronomy 14–15

NEW INSIGHTS

FURTHER QUESTIONS

PERSONAL PRAYERS

HISTORICAL CONTEXT

The Israelites remained encamped on the plains of Moab, across the Jordan, east of Canaan, in 1407 BC as they awaited God's direction to enter the Promised Land. The first five books of the Bible, called the Pentateuch, were written by the prophet Moses from approximately 1446–1406 BC.

LAW AND GOSPEL THEMES

Three feasts were to be celebrated by all of Israel each year: Passover (remembering the Passover in Egypt, March/April); the Feast of Weeks, also called Pentecost in the Septuagint, the Greek translation of the Old Testament (seven weeks after the first grain harvest, May/June); and the Feast of Booths, also called the Succoth (after the final harvest, September/October). All of Israel was to gather in a central location for these feasts, keeping them united. The feasts focused on God's deliverance and providence. An earthly king for Israel was NOT God's idea. Deuteronomy 18:15–19 points to a greater Prophet, Jesus. Prophets primarily "forth-told" God's Word more than foretold. Laws for civil order especially focused on marriage God's way (one man to one woman for life) and preserving the family (see the example of Deuteronomy 24:5 about the newly married man and one year off military service).

WEEKLY MEMORY VERSE

Deuteronomy 18:18, "I will raise up for them a prophet like you from among their brothers. And I will put My words in His mouth, and He shall speak to them all that I command Him."

LIFE APPLICATION STARTERS

What festivals in our worship life correspond to Passover and the Feast of Weeks? What third festival is a focal point in our worship life? How do our festivals maintain a similar focus to the originals? How do they differ? How do earthly kings still fail us? Are there prophets today? Are these civil laws on marriage and family still relevant? Are other civil laws in this section still useful to us?

PRAYER STARTERS

Pray to remember God's acts of deliverance and providence in our festival worship; that all Christians will be united and strengthened through corporate worship; for faithful prophets of God's Word; and for godly order and health in marriage, family, and society.

DAILY READINGS AND NOTES

MONDAY	TUESDAY	WEDNESDAY
Deuteronomy 16–17	Deuteronomy 18–19	Deuteronomy 20–21

THURSDAY	FRIDAY	SATURDAY
Deuteronomy 22–23	Deuteronomy 24	Deuteronomy 25–26

NEW INSIGHTS

FURTHER QUESTIONS

PERSONAL PRAYERS

HISTORICAL CONTEXT

The Israelites remained encamped on the plains of Moab, across the Jordan, east of Canaan, in 1407 BC as they awaited God's direction to enter the Promised Land. The first five books of the Bible, called the Pentateuch, were written by the prophet Moses from approximately 1446–1406 BC.

LAW AND GOSPEL THEMES

Law and Gospel are CLEARLY laid out in this farewell sermon from Moses in chapters 27–30. A summary passage is 30:19–20. The pattern plays out, leading up to Law, 27:9–26; Gospel, 28:1–14; Law, 28:15–29:29; Gospel, 30:1–20. NOTE that this is not an explanation of HOW to be saved. This section speaks of the ways of those who HAVE BEEN saved by God's gracious activity. Israel had been delivered from slavery by God and brought to faith by the Spirit. The Israelites were to live out that faith. When they rejected it, they would fall under the Law and a curse. When they followed the Lord in faith, they would receive Gospel blessings. Chapter 31 tells of Joshua as Moses' successor. Chapter 32 is a parting song by Moses filled with Law and Gospel.

WEEKLY MEMORY VERSE

Deuteronomy 32:39, "See now that I, even I, am He, and there is no god beside Me; I kill and I make alive; I wound and I heal; and there is none that can deliver out of My hand."

LIFE APPLICATION STARTERS

We are saved, like Israel, by grace alone for Jesus' sake. Now, we are to "choose life" (30:19) by rejecting sin and walking by faith since we ARE saved. When we reject our faith, what "curses" befall us in body and spirit, both now and after death? When we continue in faith, what blessings come to us in body and spirit, both now and after death? What songs remind you of these themes of Law and Gospel?

PRAYER STARTERS

Pray to repent of efforts to save yourself by keeping the Law, to trust in Jesus alone for the free gift of salvation, to keep the Law in thanks for salvation, that blessings will be upon you as you live by faith and act in love, and for music to teach you of God's Word of Law and Gospel and keep it in your mind and heart.

DAILY READINGS AND NOTES

MONDAY	TUESDAY	WEDNESDAY
Deuteronomy 27	Deuteronomy 28	Deuteronomy 29

THURSDAY	FRIDAY	SATURDAY
Deuteronomy 30	Deuteronomy 31:1–29	Deuteronomy 31:30–32:52

NEW INSIGHTS

FURTHER QUESTIONS

PERSONAL PRAYERS

HISTORICAL CONTEXT

Deuteronomy ends with Israel in Moab, across the Jordan, east of Canaan. Joshua begins in 1407 BC with Israel crossing the Jordan to take possession of the Promised Land. The books of Joshua through Esther are called the Books of History. Joshua was written by Joshua or an unknown author from approximately 1406–1375 BC.

LAW AND GOSPEL THEMES

Deuteronomy 33 is Moses' final blessing on Israel, pointing even beyond the land of Canaan to eternity in heaven through our Lord Jesus. Moses died and was buried by the Lord in Moab in a place still unknown. The Lord commissioned and encouraged Joshua for the conquest ahead. God used a deceptive prostitute for His good purposes in the overthrowing of Jericho. The Jordan parted to grant Israel entrance into Canaan. Memorial stones and circumcision kept Israel focused on the Lord. Jericho fell by God's hand. Achan betrayed God's command and died for it.

WEEKLY MEMORY VERSE

Joshua 1:5, 7, "I will not leave you or forsake you. . . . Only be strong and very courageous, being careful to do according to all the law that Moses My servant commanded you."

LIFE APPLICATION STARTERS

Israel's Promised Land in this world was the land of Canaan. What is our "promised land" on earth? How do we possess it? Why wouldn't the Lord want Israel to know Moses' burial place? What made Moses great (see Deuteronomy 34:10)? How do God's words to Joshua in chapter 1 apply to you in your effort to lead the chosen ones into the promised land of heaven? What comfort and challenge do you find in the account of Rahab? What other ethical issues arise in the conquest of Canaan? (See *TLSB* p. 376.) How do we enter the promised land through water? What does Achan teach us about our level of devotion?

PRAYER STARTERS

Pray in thanks for the examples of Moses and Joshua, in thanks for Baptism and your certain entrance into the promised land, for courage to be fully devoted to the Lord as you face temptation, and for all to repent and receive freedom through Jesus from the Lord's destruction of evil.

DAILY READINGS AND NOTES

MONDAY	TUESDAY	WEDNESDAY
Deuteronomy 33	Deuteronomy 34	Joshua 1
THURSDAY	**FRIDAY**	**SATURDAY**
Joshua 2–3	Joshua 4:1–5:12	Joshua 5:13–7:26

NEW INSIGHTS

FURTHER QUESTIONS

PERSONAL PRAYERS

HISTORICAL CONTEXT

From 1406–1400 BC and under Joshua's command, the Israelites took control of the Promised Land, and each tribe received its allotted territory. The books of Joshua through Esther are called the Books of History. Joshua was written by Joshua or an unknown author from approximately 1406–1375 BC.

LAW AND GOSPEL THEMES

All the inhabitants of Ai were utterly destroyed and the city burned after spoils had been taken, showing the Lord's intolerance for sin. Joshua reviewed the Word of the Lord (etched in stone) for all the people, including the little ones and sojourners (8:35). Gibeon deceived Joshua and Israel's leaders as they failed to ask for counsel from the Lord. The Lord added time to the day of battle at Joshua's faithful request. All the tribes of Israel were given their allotment in the Promised Land. Tiny Benjamin received the heartland of Israel, including Jerusalem. Conquest of the land required patience.

WEEKLY MEMORY VERSE

Joshua 8:35, "There was not a word of all that Moses commanded that Joshua did not read before all the assembly of Israel, and the women, and the little ones, and the sojourners who lived among them."

LIFE APPLICATION STARTERS

How is the Lord's total destruction of sinners still a threat today? How are we spared? Why is it significant that even "the little ones, and the sojourners" were present for the reading of God's Word? What do you learn from Gibeon in chapter 9? What lesson does Joshua teach you about the power of prayer in chapter 10? Will heaven have a place for you? For everyone who is a child of Abraham through faith in Jesus? Benjamin's inheritance reminds us that the Lord cares for the weak and lowly. Does God's slowness mean He is not delivering?

PRAYER STARTERS

Pray to be faithful and free from the threat of hell; that all, including children and converts to Christianity, would be able to hear God's Word and be blessed; for faithfulness in prayer for all things; to be humble and trusting even when weak; and for patience as you await the Lord's deliverance.

DAILY READINGS AND NOTES

MONDAY	TUESDAY	WEDNESDAY
Joshua 8–9	Joshua 10	Joshua 11–12
THURSDAY	**FRIDAY**	**SATURDAY**
Joshua 13–15	Joshua 16–17	Joshua 18–19

NEW INSIGHTS

FURTHER QUESTIONS

PERSONAL PRAYERS

HISTORICAL CONTEXT

Israel continued its conquest of the Promised Land between 1400–1375 BC, and then Joshua died. Judges picks up from 1380–1370 BC with troubles that befall the Israelites as they fail to fully drive out the godless inhabitants of the Promised Land. The books of Joshua through Esther are called the Books of History. The author of Judges is unknown, and the book was written in approximately 1000 BC.

LAW AND GOSPEL THEMES

The tribes living east of the Jordan built an altar to remind the Israelites of their unity, but it was first seen as an act of rebellion (see *TLSB* p. 376 for an explanation of divine warfare). Joshua renewed the commitment of him and his house to God's covenant and called on all Israel to do the same. Israel's key downfall, made clear in Judges, was its recurring rejection of God. Judges 2:10 summarizes such rejection, saying the new generation of Israel "did not know the Lord or the work that He had done for Israel." Yet God graciously rescued Israel over and over through His chosen judges.

WEEKLY MEMORY VERSE

Joshua 24:15, "And if it is evil in your eyes to serve the LORD, choose this day whom you will serve, whether the gods your fathers served in the region beyond the River, or the gods of the Amorites. . . . But as for me and my house, we will serve the LORD."

LIFE APPLICATION STARTERS

How do misunderstandings threaten the unity of your family and your church, and how do you overcome them? How well is the head of your household or congregation setting the tone for the faith of the whole family or congregation? How does the spiritual failure of one generation impact the next? How do you prevent it? Who is your Judge, who saves you from your repeated rebellion against the Lord?

PRAYER STARTERS

Pray for patience to listen to others to prevent conflict; to regularly pass on faith to the next generation in the home; for the whole church to unite in teaching faith to all its children; for preservation from moral lapses as we follow our own selfish ways; and in thanks for grace and especially for Jesus, our ultimate Judge and Savior.

DAILY READINGS AND NOTES

MONDAY	TUESDAY	WEDNESDAY
Joshua 20–21	Joshua 22	Joshua 23

THURSDAY	FRIDAY	SATURDAY
Joshua 24	Judges 1	Judges 2

NEW INSIGHTS

FURTHER QUESTIONS

PERSONAL PRAYERS

HISTORICAL CONTEXT

From 1370–1040, the Israelites continued to turn from the Lord in the newly received Promised Land, but He raised up judges to deliver them. The books of Joshua through Esther are called the Books of History. The author of Judges is unknown, and the book was written in approximately 1000 BC.

LAW AND GOSPEL THEMES

The repeated refrain of condemnation in this section is "Israel did what was evil in the sight of the Lord." It's part of the historical cycle over and over in Judges: 1) Israel strays, 2) foreign powers come to oppress, 3) Israel cries to the Lord to deliver it, and 4) the Lord provides a judge (NOT the courtroom kind but a savior to lead and deliver). Each judge was a type of Jesus, the greatest Savior. Fittingly, the Lord used a humble woman, Jael, to destroy mighty Sisera. Songs of praise were due to the Lord. Fearful Gideon received two clear signs of support from God. Jephthah made a foolish vow. Samson fell, repented, and was raised to deliverance one last time.

WEEKLY MEMORY VERSE

Judges 6:14, "And the Lord turned to [Gideon] and said, 'Go in this might of yours and save Israel from the hand of Midian; do not I send you?'"

LIFE APPLICATION STARTERS

How often do you do evil in the sight of the Lord and are only spared from destruction by God's mercy? What should you learn from Israel's experiences in Judges? Is anyone too weak to serve the Lord in mighty ways? How often do the mighty (you, at times) fall in their pride? How do you "sing" in praise to Jesus? Have you ever "laid out a fleece" for God to speak to you? Should you? Page 403 of *TLSB* gives a great reminder of our true identity. How is this identity needed today in a culture saturated with sex, humanism, politics, and so on?

PRAYER STARTERS

Pray to learn from history so you don't repeat its cycle of sin; to be strong in the Lord and humble in self; that praise to God will fill your life; to see God's signs, especially in Scripture, and know His will; and in thanks for your baptismal identity in Jesus.

DAILY READINGS AND NOTES

MONDAY	TUESDAY	WEDNESDAY
Judges 3	Judges 4–5	Judges 6–8
THURSDAY	**FRIDAY**	**SATURDAY**
Judges 9–10	Judges 11–12	Judges 13–16

NEW INSIGHTS

FURTHER QUESTIONS

PERSONAL PRAYERS

HISTORICAL CONTEXT

The Israelites displayed their great evil in the Promised Land in Judges 17–21, around the fourteenth century BC. Ruth and her benefactor, Boaz, showed rare faith in Israel in the book of Ruth, set in the eleventh century BC. Samuel was born to the tribe of Levi as the final, faithful judge (around 1080 BC). The books of Joshua through Esther are called the Books of History. The author of Ruth is unknown, and the book was written in approximately 1000 BC. The book of 1 Samuel was written in approximately 970 BC, and its author is unknown.

LAW AND GOSPEL THEMES

Micah was an Israelite, but he illustrated the rejection of the Lord so common among the people now in the Promised Land as he set up an idol and ordained a Levite to be his priest, doing "what was right in his own eyes" (Judges 17:6; cf. 21:25). The tribe of Dan compounded the evil by stealing the idol and taking the false priest to be their own. The men of the tribe of Benjamin showed their terrible evil against a Levite and his concubine, inciting warfare with the rest of Israel and leading to the deaths of tens of thousands and further sin. Ruth, a Moabite, showed tremendous faith and was grafted into the tree of Israel, leading to Jesus. She was "redeemed" by Boaz, who points to the role of Jesus. Samuel was set aside as a clear type of Jesus, acting as a priest, prophet, and kingmaker.

WEEKLY MEMORY VERSE

Ruth 1:16, "For where you go I will go, and where you lodge I will lodge. Your people shall be my people, and your God my God."

LIFE APPLICATION STARTERS

What similarities do you see between Israel in the period of the judges and America today? To what degree is the Christian Church (and you) also guilty? What should we learn and follow from Ruth and Boaz? What are you willing to give to the Lord in thanks for His blessings (consider Hannah)?

PRAYER STARTERS

Pray to be preserved from the terrible sin that befell the nation of Israel in the days of the judges, to humbly seek the Lord's power as you stand up for what is right in His sight, for faith like Ruth, for compassion like Boaz, and for commitment and thankfulness to God like Hannah.

DAILY READINGS AND NOTES

MONDAY	TUESDAY	WEDNESDAY
Judges 17–18	Judges 19–20	Judges 21
THURSDAY	**FRIDAY**	**SATURDAY**
Ruth 1–2	Ruth 3–4	1 Samuel 1

NEW INSIGHTS

FURTHER QUESTIONS

PERSONAL PRAYERS

HISTORICAL CONTEXT

Samuel was born to the tribe of Levi as the final, faithful judge, serving from approximately 1080–1049 BC, just before Saul became the first king of Israel. The books of Joshua through Esther are called the Books of History. The book of 1 Samuel was written in approximately 970 BC, and its author is unknown.

LAW AND GOSPEL THEMES

Words are important. Vows are not to be broken. Hannah lived by this and praised the Lord with her words. Eli and his sons forgot their vows and bore God's curse. Samuel committed to following the Word of the Lord and grew "both in stature and in favor with the Lord and also with man." (2:26) He answered God's call in faith. Faithless Israel fell to the hands of the Philistines, losing the ark of the covenant as they trusted in it as a mere good luck charm. Samuel pointed Israel to the Lord, but they demanded a king so that they might be "like all the nations" (8:5). Rather than relying on God, they wanted a king to fight for them. God condemned their sin and cursed them by giving them what they wanted. Still, God never abandoned His chosen people.

WEEKLY MEMORY VERSE

1 Samuel 2:1–2, "My heart exults in the LORD; my horn is exalted in the LORD. My mouth derides my enemies, because I rejoice in Your salvation. There is none holy like the LORD: there is none besides You; there is no rock like our God."

LIFE APPLICATION STARTERS

Do you keep your word of promise to others? To God? Consider your confirmation vow to remain faithful to all God's Word and Sacraments, even to the point of death. How is your family or church like Eli and his sons? How is your family or church like Elkanah, Hannah, and Samuel? What should politicians and citizens today learn from this week's readings (consider authority, use of force, responsibility, etc.)?

PRAYER STARTERS

Pray to trust in the promises of the Lord, to keep your vows to God and man, that you would praise the Lord always as you reflect on His constant faithfulness, for families and congregations to be united in love, for courage to rebuke evil, for faithful government that submits to God's ultimate control, and that you would not go along with the sinful crowd.

DAILY READINGS AND NOTES

MONDAY	TUESDAY	WEDNESDAY
1 Samuel 2	1 Samuel 3	1 Samuel 4

THURSDAY	FRIDAY	SATURDAY
1 Samuel 5:1–7:2	1 Samuel 7:3–17	1 Samuel 8

NEW INSIGHTS

FURTHER QUESTIONS

PERSONAL PRAYERS

HISTORICAL CONTEXT

We pick up this week from around 1049–1031 BC, when Saul became king of Israel and Samuel delivered the word of the Lord to them. The books of Joshua through Esther are called the Books of History. The book of 1 Samuel was written in approximately 970 BC, and its author is unknown.

LAW AND GOSPEL THEMES

The Lord chose Saul from the tiny Matrite clan of the tiny tribe of Benjamin to be king over Israel. Saul was fearful and even tried to hide. Some rejected Saul as king because he seemed too weak. With God's power, Saul led Israel to unite and defeat the Ammonites. Saul showed mercy to his opponents in Israel. With a weather sign from God, Samuel spoke judgment and promise to Israel before he died. In spite of their sin, God would graciously forgive. Saul offered a burnt offering against God's will and started down a selfish path that led to self-destruction. The people ransomed Jonathan from Saul's rash vow. The word *regret* is used to describe God choosing Saul to show us God's sorrow over our sinful rebellion, not to imply that He made a mistake. He still knows all things and works all things for our ultimate good.

WEEKLY MEMORY VERSE

1 Samuel 12:24, "Only fear the Lord and serve Him faithfully with all your heart. For consider what great things He has done for you."

LIFE APPLICATION STARTERS

In what ways are you like Saul—fearful to follow God's call, quick to become puffed up, self-reliant, penitent, rash, disobedient? How is God merciful and gracious with you as He was with Saul? Where do you find prophetic words to guide you in God's way? Does God ever need to "regret" His call on your life? Like Israel for Jonathan, who has ransomed you from God's just wrath?

PRAYER STARTERS

Pray for courage to follow God in His ways, even when they seem too hard for you; to listen to those whom God has chosen, even though they may seem weak, especially our Savior, Jesus, who appeared weak upon the cross yet was still almighty God; that you do not make foolish vows; to ransom the mistreated; and for faithfulness lest you lose the favor of the Lord.

DAILY READINGS AND NOTES

MONDAY	TUESDAY	WEDNESDAY
1 Samuel 9–10	1 Samuel 11	1 Samuel 12

THURSDAY	FRIDAY	SATURDAY
1 Samuel 13	1 Samuel 14	1 Samuel 15

NEW INSIGHTS

FURTHER QUESTIONS

PERSONAL PRAYERS

HISTORICAL CONTEXT

From approximately 1031–1010 BC, Saul moved further from the Lord, and David rose up in his place as king. The books of Joshua through Esther are called the Books of History. The book of 1 Samuel was written in approximately 970 BC, and its author is unknown.

LAW AND GOSPEL THEMES

Samuel was grieved over Saul's rebellion and was hesitant to move ahead. The Lord directed Samuel to His continued grace that would then be revealed through David. The Lord sometimes allows evil so His ultimate good might be fulfilled (see 1 Samuel 16:14). Small David acted with the mighty power of God to defeat Goliath. Deep friendships sustain the Lord's faithful children, as seen through David and Jonathan. Jealousy is a destructive force. Saul worked and plotted for David's death to no avail, since God was on David's side. Even though David was God's chosen deliverer, he still would suffer many trials along the way. Yet God protected, empowered, and used David for the good of Israel.

WEEKLY MEMORY VERSE

1 Samuel 17:37, "And David said, 'The Lord who delivered me from the paw of the lion and from the paw of the bear will deliver me from the hand of this Philistine.'"

LIFE APPLICATION STARTERS

How have you become frozen in your path as you regret the past? How has the Lord used evil situations in your life to draw you closer to Him and down better paths? Who do you rely on to speak up for you and keep you from despair when evil comes your way? What giants are you afraid to face? What does David's life teach you about perseverance? What does Saul teach you about betrayal from those whom you think you should be able to trust? In whom alone should you fully trust?

PRAYER STARTERS

Pray for courage to move ahead and leave your regrets in the hands of the Lord; to be preserved from the assaults of Satan and his demons; to courageously go wherever God leads you; to be a true and trustworthy friend by the power of the Lord; and to fix your eyes on Jesus as your trustworthy Savior always.

DAILY READINGS AND NOTES

MONDAY	TUESDAY	WEDNESDAY
1 Samuel 16	1 Samuel 17	1 Samuel 18–19

THURSDAY	FRIDAY	SATURDAY
1 Samuel 20–21	1 Samuel 22	1 Samuel 23

NEW INSIGHTS

FURTHER QUESTIONS

PERSONAL PRAYERS

HISTORICAL CONTEXT

In the span of 1010–1009 BC, Samuel died, Saul continued his steady fall toward his own death, and David rose in power. The books of Joshua through Esther are called the Books of History. The books of 1 and 2 Samuel were originally one long document that was later divided. The book of 1 Samuel was written in approximately 970 BC, and its author is unknown.

LAW AND GOSPEL THEMES

David acted mercifully toward Saul as the Lord's anointed, even though his men advised vengeance. Saul battled between good and evil but still relied on his own power. A faithful wife, Abigail, protected her foolish husband, Nabal, from David's wrath but could not protect him from God's judgment. David was able to forgive Saul by the Spirit's power. God was silent to rebellious Saul, so he sinfully turned to the medium of En-dor, who called up Samuel from the dead. Saul received only the prediction of his death to come the next day. When David's wives and many other women and children were captured, he "strengthened himself in the LORD his God" (1 Samuel 30:6). Even though Saul died in disgrace, his people still honored him as the Lord's anointed.

WEEKLY MEMORY VERSE

1 Samuel 30:6, "But David strengthened himself in the LORD his God."

LIFE APPLICATION STARTERS

Are you able to show mercy to those who hate you and harm you, even if they do it repeatedly? By what power can you show such mercy? What does Abigail teach about the roles of a faithful wife and woman of God? What will come to all who call on sorcery or any other power besides the Lord? How should we treat God's chosen servants, including our elected officials?

PRAYER STARTERS

Pray for the strength to be merciful, even to those who persistently harm you; in thanks for godly women who protect foolish men from their self-destruction; to never give in to the temptation to call upon evil powers; to always receive your strength from the Lord; and for all who are called as servants of the Lord.

DAILY READINGS AND NOTES

MONDAY	TUESDAY	WEDNESDAY
1 Samuel 24	1 Samuel 25	1 Samuel 26

THURSDAY	FRIDAY	SATURDAY
1 Samuel 27–29	1 Samuel 30	1 Samuel 31

NEW INSIGHTS

FURTHER QUESTIONS

PERSONAL PRAYERS

HISTORICAL CONTEXT

Saul had just died. David was anointed king of Judah and then of all Israel. His reign prospered from approximately 1009–970 BC, as he was faithful to the Lord. The books of Joshua through Esther are called the Books of History. 1 and 2 Samuel were originally one long document that was later divided. The book of 2 Samuel was written in approximately 970 BC, and its author is unknown.

LAW AND GOSPEL THEMES

David's response to Saul's assisted suicide showed great respect for God's anointed and for life (2 Samuel 1:14). David would not delight in the destruction of his enemies, especially within Israel. In-fighting hurt both sides (as seen in Abner vs. Joab etc.). We are not to get revenge on those who wrong us or avenge those we love (3:26–30). David corrupted himself by marrying Jebusite wives (5:13). Uzzah was struck dead when he took hold of the ark of the covenant, which was wrongly being moved on a cart rather than being carried by Levites (6:6–7). Lesson learned. After three months, the ark was carried to Jerusalem with rejoicing (6:13). David honored God properly, even if Michal was offended (6:20–23). David's promised "house" from God would not be a building but an eternal dynasty in Jesus (7:16).

WEEKLY MEMORY VERSE

2 Samuel 6:21, "I will celebrate before the Lord."

LIFE APPLICATION STARTERS

What does David's godly attitude about the death of Saul teach us about the practices of assisted suicide and euthanasia? Who should take care of vengeance against evil? How does in-fighting hurt your family? Your church? What items today are holy? How should you treat holy items? If your worship practice aligns with God's will, how should you respond to the criticism of others? Is David's "house" enduring?

PRAYER STARTERS

Pray that you will respect and defend ALL life, for God to have mercy on our enemies and heal our divisions, for unity in the Body of Christ, that you properly honor the holy things of God and worship without fear, and in thanks for Jesus as your lasting temple.

DAILY READINGS AND NOTES

MONDAY	TUESDAY	WEDNESDAY
2 Samuel 1–2	2 Samuel 3–4	2 Samuel 5
THURSDAY	**FRIDAY**	**SATURDAY**
2 Samuel 6	2 Samuel 7	2 Samuel 8–10

NEW INSIGHTS

FURTHER QUESTIONS

PERSONAL PRAYERS

HISTORICAL CONTEXT

Between approximately 1002–970 BC, David continued his reign over all Israel, fell into sin, lost control to his son Absalom, and regained it, partially, again. The books of Joshua through Esther are called the Books of History. 1 and 2 Samuel were originally one long document that was later divided. The book of 2 Samuel was written in approximately 970 BC, and its author is unknown.

LAW AND GOSPEL THEMES

David failed to carry out his vocation as king, staying at home in security and falling into adultery, deceit, and murder. David repented of his sins and was freely forgiven, but there were terrible and lasting consequences. David's son, Amnon, followed his father's sexual sin against his stepsister Tamar. Absalom wrongly took God's authority and murdered his brother Amnon. David failed to discipline Absalom properly, neither condemning nor pardoning him. Absalom turned further from the Lord and took the kingdom from David. David reclaimed the kingdom but lost Absalom. David showed mercy to his enemies, both in Israel and beyond, but still faced opposition and bloodshed. Yet David's heart remained true to the Lord as he sang in praise to Him.

WEEKLY MEMORY VERSE

2 Samuel 22:2–3, "The Lord is my rock and my fortress and my deliverer, my God, my rock, in whom I take refuge, my shield, and the horn of my salvation."

LIFE APPLICATION STARTERS

When have you failed to follow your God-given vocations and it resulted in falling into sin? How does a failure to fully discipline children result in ongoing evil consequences for David, for you, for a nation? What can you learn from David about the proper response to a godly rebuke (see 2 Samuel 12:13; 16:10; 19:8)? Should you expect life on earth to get easier for you if you're faithful to the Lord?

PRAYER STARTERS

Pray to fulfill your God-given vocations, keep busy, and be preserved from temptations; to admit your sin when rebuked and flee to God for forgiveness; to have wisdom and courage in disciplining the next generations, showing godly judgment and mercy; and to persevere in faith in spite of continued attacks by Satan, the world, and yourself.

DAILY READINGS AND NOTES

MONDAY	TUESDAY	WEDNESDAY
2 Samuel 11–12	2 Samuel 13:1–14:24	2 Samuel 14:25–16:23
THURSDAY	**FRIDAY**	**SATURDAY**
2 Samuel 17–18	2 Samuel 19–20	2 Samuel 21–22

NEW INSIGHTS

FURTHER QUESTIONS

PERSONAL PRAYERS

HISTORICAL CONTEXT

The book of 2 Samuel ends with the final exploits of King David (ca. 970 BC). The book of 1 Kings picks up with the anointing of Solomon as king of all Israel and tells of his wisdom and accomplishments during his reign from 971–932 BC. The books of Joshua through Esther are called the Books of History. The books of 1 and 2 Kings were originally one long document that was later divided. The book of 1 Kings was written in approximately 560 BC, and its author is unknown.

LAW AND GOSPEL THEMES

David spoke an oracle at the end of his reign that expressed his faith in God's eternal covenant promises. Still, David reverted to pride and trust in might again as he celebrated his warriors and took a census, bringing a curse on Israel . . . until he fled back to God for mercy. David's spoiled son, Adonijah, set himself up as king above the brother God had chosen to succeed David (1 Chronicles 22:9–10), but God's plan was not confounded. Solomon took his rightful throne and preserved the line to Jesus. Solomon received the wisdom he sought from God but still acted foolishly as he acquired wives and wealth that distracted him. The temple united Israel in worship of the Lord and pointed ahead to the sacrifice to end all sacrifices: Jesus.

WEEKLY MEMORY VERSE

1 Kings 8:23, "O Lord, God of Israel, there is no God like You, in heaven above or on earth beneath, keeping covenant and showing steadfast love to Your servants who walk before You with all their heart."

LIFE APPLICATION STARTERS

How does David's life reflect the tendency of success to lead to a fall? Have you seen this in your life? Why are God's gifts of mercy and grace more important than his gifts of wisdom, wealth, and might? Sacrifices on Mount Moriah (by Abraham, David, and Solomon) point ahead to which greater sacrifice on nearby Mount Calvary that blesses you? How does Solomon focus on God's care for the Gentiles, including most Christians today (see 1 Kings 8:43, 60)?

PRAYER STARTERS

Pray that you will never trust in your own wisdom and might more than God's mercy and grace, to share proper Law and Gospel with your family and be spared from the curse of sin, and to honor God with your greatest sacrifices and boldly take on His mission of salvation for the world.

DAILY READINGS AND NOTES

MONDAY	TUESDAY	WEDNESDAY
2 Samuel 23	2 Samuel 24	1 Kings 1–2

THURSDAY	FRIDAY	SATURDAY
1 Kings 3–4	1 Kings 5–7	1 Kings 8

NEW INSIGHTS

FURTHER QUESTIONS

PERSONAL PRAYERS

HISTORICAL CONTEXT

When Solomon's reign came to an end, Israel was divided and ruled by separate kings from then onward. This week, we read about the kings Asa and Ahab, spanning around 947–853 BC. The books of Joshua through Esther are called the Books of History. The books of 1 and 2 Kings were originally one long document that was later divided. The book of 1 Kings was written in approximately 560 BC, and its author is unknown.

LAW AND GOSPEL THEMES

The Lord consecrated the temple built by Solomon. However, he warned that if Israel turned from the Lord, it would "become a heap of ruins" (1 Kings 9:8). Foreigners like the queen of Sheba were drawn to Solomon's wisdom so he could teach them of the Lord. Yet pagan women drew Solomon away from the Lord. Due to Solomon's sin, his son inherited a divided kingdom. Death was as sleep—only temporary—for the Lord's faithful (11:43). Elijah's raising of the widow's son reinforces this (see 17:22). Kings come and go, but the Word of the Lord endures with its curses and blessings. Grace can break patterns of evil (see 15:14). God gives courage and victory against the greatest of evil, as He did for Elijah in chapter 18.

WEEKLY MEMORY VERSE

1 Kings 11:43, "And Solomon slept with his fathers and was buried in the city of David his father."

LIFE APPLICATION STARTERS

Buildings mean nothing if there is no faith in the Lord. How should you apply this? How do you walk the balance of interacting with the world to be a witness for Jesus without being pulled into sin by the world? What's best to pass on or receive as an inheritance—money, houses, toys, skills, power, a great name, knowledge? How permanent is death? How can you be sure?

PRAYER STARTERS

Pray to offer up all you build to the glory of God; to never turn from the Word of the Lord or fail to live by it; that you will be a godly witness to all; that you will resist the sin of all the ungodly; to be courageous and victorious (at least in spiritual terms) in the face of evil enemies, no matter how great; and to await your resurrection with hope, confidence, and joy.

DAILY READINGS AND NOTES

MONDAY	TUESDAY	WEDNESDAY
1 Kings 9–10	1 Kings 11	1 Kings 12

THURSDAY	FRIDAY	SATURDAY
1 Kings 13–14	1 Kings 15–16	1 Kings 17–18

NEW INSIGHTS

FURTHER QUESTIONS

PERSONAL PRAYERS

HISTORICAL CONTEXT

The prophets Elijah, Micaiah, and Elisha served in the Northern Kingdom of Israel under kings Ahab, Ahaziah, and Jehoram. Pious King Jehoshaphat reigned over the Southern Kingdom of Judah (ca. 870–850 BC). The books of Joshua through Esther are called the Books of History. The books of 1 and 2 Kings were originally one long document that was later divided. The books of 1 and 2 Kings were written in approximately 560 BC, and their author is unknown.

LAW AND GOSPEL THEMES

Elijah defeated the prophets of Baal, yet he was terrified by the threats of evil Queen Jezebel and fled for his life, complaining that he alone remained faithful. At Mount Horeb (where Moses received the Ten Commandments), in grace, the Lord strengthened Elijah through a still, small voice. Elisha left everything behind as he was called by the Lord to succeed Elijah, who was miraculously taken up to heaven. God was merciful to Ahab, but his persistent sin finally led to his demise. Ahab's son followed his sinful lead, entering a foolish war with Moab. Elisha performed several miracles by God's power, including raising a dead boy and healing leprous Naaman, a Syrian. A miracle of oil was cut short by the widow's limited faith . . . and vessels to hold the oil.

WEEKLY MEMORY VERSE

2 Kings 2:11, "And as they still went on and talked, behold, chariots of fire and horses of fire separated the two of them. And Elijah went up by a whirlwind into heaven."

LIFE APPLICATION STARTERS

When have you felt alone in your faith? How has God reminded you that you are never alone? When and how has God's still, small voice spoken most clearly to you? What have you left behind to follow the Lord? How can you honor God for His mercy to you? What comfort and guidance do you receive from Elisha's miracles?

PRAYER STARTERS

Pray to resist Satan's lies that say you are alone in faith; to hear God's voice, especially in His Word in Scripture; that you do not take God's mercy for granted but praise Him with new obedience; to pass to the next generation faith like Elijah versus sin like Ahab; and to see God's miracles for and through us still today.

DAILY READINGS AND NOTES

MONDAY	TUESDAY	WEDNESDAY
1 Kings 19	1 Kings 20	1 Kings 21–22

THURSDAY	FRIDAY	SATURDAY
2 Kings 1–2	2 Kings 3–4	2 Kings 5

NEW INSIGHTS

FURTHER QUESTIONS

PERSONAL PRAYERS

HISTORICAL CONTEXT

Elisha carried on his faithful service as prophet in Israel. Several evil kings reigned over the Northern Kingdom of Israel, moving them steadily to their pending fall and exile in 722 BC. Judah also toyed with evil, though Joash shone as a godly king in the years 835–796 BC. The books of Joshua through Esther are called the Books of History. The books of 1 and 2 Kings were originally one long document that was later divided. The book of 2 Kings was written in approximately 560 BC, and its author is unknown.

LAW AND GOSPEL THEMES

Elisha showed his servant that the forces serving the Lord are always greater than those of evil as horses and chariots of fire were revealed (2 Kings 6:17). Israel's suffering for its evil was terrible as the people faithlessly resorted to cannibalism (6:29). Such judgment was the result of man's rebellion, not God's lack of care. The Lord delivers without our help and proclaims victory through weak vessels (see ch. 7). Elisha wept over the coming destruction of Israel by Syria (see 8:7–13). Cunning Jehu brought God's wrath to Israel, including destroying Jezebel and the prophets of Baal. Jehoash, guided by the priest Jehoiada, repaired the temple in Jerusalem. Ahaz ruled with evil in Judah, but Isaiah (we hear later) gave him a prophecy of Jesus' coming (Isaiah 7:10–14).

WEEKLY MEMORY VERSE

2 Kings 6:16, "Do not be afraid, for those who are with us are more than those who are with them."

LIFE APPLICATION STARTERS

When have you seen a glimpse of God's invisible power that is greater than all evil? When have you blamed God or His messengers for evil that has come upon you? Are you capable of serving for the Lord's good purposes? Do you ever grieve over the coming destruction of all evil on Judgment Day?

PRAYER STARTERS

Pray for eyes of faith to see that God's power is always greater than evil, to repent of your sin rather than blaming God for the evil that befalls you, that God would use you to deliver His words of Law and Gospel despite your weakness, and that all sinners who are facing destruction on Judgment Day would repent and receive free salvation in Jesus.

DAILY READINGS AND NOTES

MONDAY	TUESDAY	WEDNESDAY
2 Kings 6–7	2 Kings 8	2 Kings 9–10

THURSDAY	FRIDAY	SATURDAY
2 Kings 11–12	2 Kings 13–14	2 Kings 15–16

NEW INSIGHTS

FURTHER QUESTIONS

PERSONAL PRAYERS

HISTORICAL CONTEXT

The book of 2 Kings covers events from approximately 852–561 BC. After the death of Elisha and the reign of many godless kings, the Northern Kingdom came to its destruction in 722 BC. Judah, despite some relatively faithful kings, fell in 587 BC. The books of Joshua through Esther are called the Books of History. The books of 1 and 2 Kings were originally one long document that was later divided. The book of 2 Kings was written in approximately 560 BC, and its author is unknown.

LAW AND GOSPEL THEMES

Exile came to the Northern Kingdom because they "sinned against the LORD their God, who had brought them up out of the land of Egypt" (2 Kings 17:7). The maps and notes on pages 609 and 615 of *TLSB* summarize well the exiles of Israel and Judah, respectively. Under Assyrian control, foreigners settled in Israel and became the ancestors of the Samaritans in Jesus' day—bringing false religion with them. Hezekiah did good in Judah but was callous about the pending fall of Judah under his son, Manasseh, who was the worst king in Judah's history. Josiah became king at eight years old and served well under the guidance of Hilkiah, the high priest. Solomon's temple was destroyed by Babylon in 587 BC.

WEEKLY MEMORY VERSE

2 Kings 19:6, "Thus says the LORD: Do not be afraid because of the words that you have heard, with which the servants of the king of Assyria have reviled Me."

LIFE APPLICATION STARTERS

What exile has fallen upon you as a result of your rebellion against the Lord? What foreign religion or false gods have you allowed to corrupt your belief in the Lord? If God can make the earth spin backward, what is there He cannot do for you? Do you have proper concern for the generations that will follow you? How important are wise teachers for children?

PRAYER STARTERS

Pray to humbly repent and follow the Lord before you fall into exile; that your faith, based on pure teaching from God's Word, will never be corrupted; to seek to pass along sincere faith and better blessings to the next generations, teaching them to know the LORD; and to trust in God's almighty power to guide and bless you.

DAILY READINGS AND NOTES

MONDAY	TUESDAY	WEDNESDAY
2 Kings 17	2 Kings 18–19	2 Kings 20

THURSDAY	FRIDAY	SATURDAY
2 Kings 21	2 Kings 22–23	2 Kings 24–25

NEW INSIGHTS

FURTHER QUESTIONS

PERSONAL PRAYERS

HISTORICAL CONTEXT

The author of both 1 and 2 Chronicles, which was originally one long document, is likely a Levite who lived among the Israelites after they returned to Jerusalem from Babylonian captivity. The two books review history from the time of Adam to the decree of Cyrus, king of Persia, in 538 BC, which allowed the people to return to rebuild the temple. This week, we review the genealogies leading up to David and through the first part of his life, up to around 1000 BC. The books of Joshua through Esther are called the Books of History. The books of 1 and 2 Chronicles were written in approximately 430 BC.

LAW AND GOSPEL THEMES

Chapters 1–9 feature genealogies from Adam (the father of all nations) to all Israel; to Judah, Benjamin, and Levi; and then to the exiles returned from Babylon. These genealogies show God's plan of salvation for all people as His Gospel care delivers from the Law's condemnation. Extra focus is given to the Levites at the center of the record to show that life and salvation come to all people of all times through the ministry of God's Word and worship. Music is key in such worship. Tiny David was lifted up as king by God's grace, as reflected in his life, music, and prayer.

WEEKLY MEMORY VERSE

1 Chronicles 17:9, "And I will appoint a place for My people Israel and will plant them, that they may dwell in their own place and be disturbed no more."

LIFE APPLICATION STARTERS

How do you still see God's hand in the genealogies traced through history? What evidence do you see that nations and families thrive when God's Word and worship are at the center of life and suffer when they are not? What can you do to support and find new ministers to lead the worship of God? How does music convey God's Word of Law and Gospel in worship?

PRAYER STARTERS

Pray for faithfulness to God's Word and worship throughout generations; to pass along the importance of God's Word, worship, and music to all children in public and home gatherings; for the support of ministers; and that new servants will answer God's call to lead us in ongoing public worship.

DAILY READINGS AND NOTES

MONDAY	TUESDAY	WEDNESDAY
1 Chronicles 1–4	1 Chronicles 5–8	1 Chronicles 9–12

THURSDAY	FRIDAY	SATURDAY
1 Chronicles 13–14	1 Chronicles 15–16	1 Chronicles 17

NEW INSIGHTS

FURTHER QUESTIONS

PERSONAL PRAYERS

HISTORICAL CONTEXT

The author of both 1 and 2 Chronicles, which was originally one long document, is likely a Levite who lived among the Israelites after they returned to Jerusalem from Babylonian captivity. This author recorded the events of the latter part of King David's life up until his death in 969 BC. The books of Joshua through Esther are called the Books of History. The books of 1 and 2 Chronicles were written in approximately 430 BC.

LAW AND GOSPEL THEMES

David's blatant sins were omitted in 1 Chronicles as they were secondary to the focus on the worship of God. Chapter 20 highlights the defeat of giants like those that kept faithless Israel from entering the Promised Land under Moses. David and Israel suffered as they counted THEIR power with a census. The focus of chapters 23–26 is David's preparation for orderly and regular worship in the temple to come, with chapter 25 emphasizing the importance of music. Chapters 28–29 focus on the passing of the kingship to Solomon. Both themes point to Jesus, who will always be the focus of worship as King of kings. In chapter 29, David teaches of proper stewardship as he joyfully gave for the future temple and encouraged all to join him in response to God's grace.

WEEKLY MEMORY VERSE

1 Chronicles 22:10, "[Solomon] shall build a house for My name. He shall be My son, and I will be his father, and I will establish his royal throne in Israel forever."

LIFE APPLICATION STARTERS

What does David teach you about the power of God in public worship versus the greatness of your sins? How are you tempted to count YOUR power and put your trust in it rather than in God? How is Jesus revealed as Prophet, Priest, and King in our public worship? How do you freely give to support public worship in response to God's grace?

PRAYER STARTERS

Pray to cherish public worship as a gift from God that keeps you focused on Him and not on yourself; to count God's blessings rather than your power; that you will always honor Jesus as the Word of God who died, rose, and rules the universe; and to freely give your time, talent, and treasure to God.

DAILY READINGS AND NOTES

MONDAY	TUESDAY	WEDNESDAY
1 Chronicles 18–20	1 Chronicles 21	1 Chronicles 22
THURSDAY	**FRIDAY**	**SATURDAY**
1 Chronicles 23–27	1 Chronicles 28	1 Chronicles 29

NEW INSIGHTS

FURTHER QUESTIONS

PERSONAL PRAYERS

HISTORICAL CONTEXT

The author of 1 and 2 Chronicles, likely a Levite who lived among the Israelites after they returned to Jerusalem from Babylonian captivity, recorded the events of the reigns of Solomon (over the united kingdom) and his son Rehoboam (over Judah) from 970–914 BC. The books of Joshua through Esther are called the Books of History. The books of 1 and 2 Chronicles, originally one long document, were written in approximately 430 BC.

LAW AND GOSPEL THEMES

The author of 2 Chronicles portrays Solomon as the ideal king over an ideal kingdom, glossing over his failures. The chronicler seeks to comfort the hurting and thus speaks prophecy of Jesus and His perfect reign forever. Solomon's reign was a witness that led Gentiles, like King Hiram of Tyre, to the LORD (2 Chronicles 2:11–12). Sacrifices on Mount Moriah by Abraham, David, and Solomon pointed to Jesus' final sacrifice in view of Moriah. The LORD's transcendent glory filled the temple, and He also ignited the sacrifices at the temple's dedication. Rehoboam, like many sinful kings, misused marriage as a means to political power (see 11:18).

WEEKLY MEMORY VERSE

2 Chronicles 2:12, "Blessed be the LORD God of Israel, who made heaven and earth, who has given King David a wise son."

LIFE APPLICATION STARTERS

How does the LORD use the good aspects of sinful Solomon's reign to point to and illustrate the coming reign of Jesus? How can a sinner like you point the eyes of all, including the Gentiles, to the Creator of the universe and His salvation? What sacrifices can you make to point eyes to Jesus? How does the LORD's glory fill our churches? How is marriage still misused for selfish gain?

PRAYER STARTERS

Pray that the LORD will forgive your failures and still use you to point all eyes to Jesus; for all people to see their Creator and Savior through the witness you bear; that you will offer right sacrifices of praise and holy living; and for marriage to be cherished as a gift from God and not a tool for selfish gain.

DAILY READINGS AND NOTES

MONDAY	TUESDAY	WEDNESDAY
2 Chronicles 1–2	2 Chronicles 3–5	2 Chronicles 6–7

THURSDAY	FRIDAY	SATURDAY
2 Chronicles 8–9	2 Chronicles 10–11	2 Chronicles 12

NEW INSIGHTS

FURTHER QUESTIONS

PERSONAL PRAYERS

HISTORICAL CONTEXT

The author of 1 and 2 Chronicles, likely a Levite who lived among the Israelites after they returned to Jerusalem from Babylonian captivity, recorded the events of the kings of Judah from Abijah (Abijam) in 914 BC to Joash in 796 BC. The books of Joshua through Esther are called the Books of History. The books of 1 and 2 Chronicles, originally one long document, were written in approximately 430 BC.

LAW AND GOSPEL THEMES

In 1 Kings, we hear of evil king Abijam, which means "my father is *Yam*," a Canaanite god. The chronicler refers to him as Abijah, which means "my father is *Yahweh*." Sadly, the first name is more fitting. Asa prospered as he purged the land of idolatry and even removed his idolatrous mother, Maacah, from her role as queen. Jehoshaphat was faithful to the LORD in many ways, especially in sending out his officials to teach the Law of the LORD. Athaliah used evil and murder to gain control of Judah, but her grandson Joash was rightly made king, and she was put to death. Joash prospered only insofar as he heeded the counsel of his wise elders.

WEEKLY MEMORY VERSE

2 Chronicles 16:9, "For the eyes of the LORD run to and fro throughout the whole earth, to give strong support to those whose heart is blameless toward Him."

LIFE APPLICATION STARTERS

What idolatry do you need to purge from your life before it pulls you further away from the LORD? What idolatry should be purged from your congregation? How do you allow family ties to inhibit your walk with the LORD? What can you do to better teach the Law of the LORD throughout our land? How might we all benefit from the wise counsel of godly elders?

PRAYER STARTERS

Pray that you recognize the idolatry in your life and get rid of it; for the courage to reject the evil counsel and ways of those who oppose the LORD, even if they're in your family; for wise elders to guide you in the way of the LORD and ears to listen; and that the Word of the LORD is taught faithfully in your home, congregation, and community.

DAILY READINGS AND NOTES

MONDAY	TUESDAY	WEDNESDAY
2 Chronicles 13–14	2 Chronicles 15–16	2 Chronicles 17–18

THURSDAY	FRIDAY	SATURDAY
2 Chronicles 19–20	2 Chronicles 21–22	2 Chronicles 23–24

NEW INSIGHTS

FURTHER QUESTIONS

PERSONAL PRAYERS

HISTORICAL CONTEXT

The author of 1 and 2 Chronicles, likely a Levite who lived among the Israelites after they returned to Jerusalem from Babylonian captivity, recorded the events of the kings of Judah from Amaziah in 796 BC to Amon in 643 BC. The books of Joshua through Esther are called the Books of History. The books of 1 and 2 Chronicles, originally one long document, were written in approximately 430 BC.

LAW AND GOSPEL THEMES

God was still in control through the reigns of kings, whether good or bad. Amaziah started off good but began to compromise on the truth in his later years, allowing idolatry throughout Judah. Uzziah (Azariah in 1 and 2 Kings) also started out as a good king, but he fell to pride and took the place of the priests by offering incense in the temple. He was struck with leprosy, so he had to leave the palace and rule to his son Jotham. Uzziah died ten years later, still leprous. Jotham learned from the good and bad example of his father and served well as king. Ahaz was notoriously wicked, closing the temple. Hezekiah restored temple worship and holy feast observance, starting with Passover. He gave due honor and care to the priests and Levites.

WEEKLY MEMORY VERSE

2 Chronicles 32:7, "Be strong and courageous. Do not be afraid or dismayed before the king of Assyria and all the horde that is with him, for there are more with us than with him."

LIFE APPLICATION STARTERS

How are we tempted to compromise on the truth as our race of faith grows long? Do we properly honor God's order in the church with due respect for those called as ministers to the Body of Christ? How do we honor God through His servants? If we are wise, what might we learn from the good and bad in our parents and other godly influences in our lives?

PRAYER STARTERS

Pray that you never compromise on the truth of God's Word but hold to it faithfully until the end of your days on earth; for due honor and care for the pastors, teachers, and other committed servants of the Lord in the church today; and for wisdom to discern between the good and bad examples we see and follow what is good.

DAILY READINGS AND NOTES

MONDAY	TUESDAY	WEDNESDAY
2 Chronicles 25–26	2 Chronicles 27–28	2 Chronicles 29

THURSDAY	FRIDAY	SATURDAY
2 Chronicles 30–31	2 Chronicles 32	2 Chronicles 33

NEW INSIGHTS

FURTHER QUESTIONS

PERSONAL PRAYERS

HISTORICAL CONTEXT

We conclude the books of 1 and 2 Chronicles, covering the reigns of Josiah (641 BC) through Zedekiah and the fall of Judah (588 BC). Hope for restoration was given by the edict of Cyrus (538 BC). Ezra, the scribe, wrote around 440 BC about the return of the exiles from Babylon and the restoration of Jerusalem through 457 BC. The books of Joshua through Esther are called the Books of History.

LAW AND GOSPEL THEMES

After Josiah's efforts to draw Judah back to the LORD failed, the people continued their steady fall from faith. Most of those in Judah were killed or taken into exile in Babylon, and the land of Judah was FORCED by the LORD to receive forty-nine years (seven by seven, for completeness) of Sabbath rest to make up for missed observance. The LORD spoke to His people through Persian King Cyrus and commanded the rebuilding of His house in Jerusalem. Non-Israelite neighbors sought to join in the rebuilding but were denied in an effort to keep the temple and its practice pure. In spite of opposition, the rebuilding project was completed. Ezra was protected as he returned to Jerusalem to teach the Law of the LORD again.

WEEKLY MEMORY VERSE

Ezra 7:9–10, "The good hand of his God was on him. For Ezra had set his heart to study the Law of the LORD, and to do it and to teach His statues and rules in Israel."

LIFE APPLICATION STARTERS

To what ends is God willing to go to draw His people back to Himself? What warning does this give to you? What comfort does the rebuilding of the temple, a type of Jesus' resurrection, give to you as you face opposition from men to God's plans? How can you follow Ezra's lead to focus on teaching God's Word?

PRAYER STARTERS

Pray for humble repentance as you face the LORD's discipline; for courage to follow the LORD, even in the face of opposition by men; that you will maintain purity of faith and worship as you also reach out to those who don't yet know the LORD; and to teach the Word of the LORD boldly.

DAILY READINGS AND NOTES

MONDAY	TUESDAY	WEDNESDAY
2 Chronicles 34–35	2 Chronicles 36	Ezra 1–2

THURSDAY	FRIDAY	SATURDAY
Ezra 3–4	Ezra 5–6	Ezra 7–8

NEW INSIGHTS

FURTHER QUESTIONS

PERSONAL PRAYERS

HISTORICAL CONTEXT

Ezra, the scribe, wrote around 440 BC about the return of the exiles from Babylon and the restoration of Jerusalem through 457 BC. Nehemiah was cupbearer to King Artaxerxes of Persia when he heard that the walls and gates of Jerusalem were still destroyed. He received the king's blessing to go and rebuild them in 445 BC. As governor of Judah, Nehemiah wrote his book between approximately 445–432 BC. The books of Joshua through Esther are called the Books of History.

LAW AND GOSPEL THEMES

Ezra, following the rebuilding of the temple, now focused on removing the corruption of Judah due to intermarriage with pagans and the adoption of their false religion. Nehemiah prayed for God's guidance in the rebuilding of Jerusalem's walls and gates. He practiced careful organization and bold, even harsh, persistence in the face of opposition. He also set a great example of generosity for the work of the Lord. Ezra stepped up again to call Judah back to obedience to the Law of the Lord as recorded in Scripture. The Judeans were moved to repentance of their sins of both omission and commission, pleading for mercy and grace.

WEEKLY MEMORY VERSE

Nehemiah 8:10, "Do not be grieved, for the joy of the Lord is your strength."

LIFE APPLICATION STARTERS

How has intermarriage between Christians and unbelievers caused harm to individuals, families, and the church? How can the lessons of Ezra address these problems today? How do prayer and wise organization fit into your efforts to serve the Lord? How should we address the sin of ignorance concerning the will of the Lord? Where is your hope in all your sin?

PRAYER STARTERS

Pray for marriages in God's way that faithfully reflect the love of Jesus to the world; to be bold in prayer in all things; to use God's gift of reason to wisely accomplish His work; and that you repent of your sin of ignorance, receive mercy, and respond in obedience.

DAILY READINGS AND NOTES

MONDAY	TUESDAY	WEDNESDAY
Ezra 9–10	Nehemiah 1	Nehemiah 2–3
THURSDAY	**FRIDAY**	**SATURDAY**
Nehemiah 4–6	Nehemiah 7–8	Nehemiah 9–10

NEW INSIGHTS

FURTHER QUESTIONS

PERSONAL PRAYERS

HISTORICAL CONTEXT

Nehemiah had guided the rebuilding of Jerusalem's walls and gates before focusing on populating it with faithful Judeans (445–433 BC). Esther acted to save the Jews in the realm of Persian King Ahasuerus (also called Xerxes). The book bearing her name covers events from approximately 483–473 BC. It was written around 400 BC by an unknown author. Job was a righteous man of God from Uz, somewhere east of Canaan. Job or one of his contemporaries likely wrote the book bearing his name somewhere in the broad range of 2200–1400 BC. The books of Joshua through Esther are called the Books of History.

LAW AND GOSPEL THEMES

Volunteers stepped up for the good of the nation as Nehemiah worked to repopulate Jerusalem. The priests and Levites led God's people in orderly worship in restored Jerusalem. Nehemiah's zeal bordered on excessive forcefulness as he accomplished God's will. Although God is never mentioned by name in Esther, His divine care is implied throughout the book. The LORD used the events of pagan politics for His good purposes. Prejudice led Haman down a path of blind vengeance and his own destruction. Esther and Mordecai celebrated their victory in the festival of Purim. Job was righteous, living by faith.

WEEKLY MEMORY VERSE

Esther 4:14, "Who knows whether you have not come to the kingdom for such a time as this?"

LIFE APPLICATION STARTERS

What sacrifices are you willing to make in volunteer service to the LORD? Should orderly worship ever be set aside? Should you be more zealous in following God's will? How do you guard against being overly forceful in your zeal? How has prejudice hurt you or the church today? Should you celebrate Purim?

PRAYER STARTERS

Pray that you will be more courageous in your volunteerism for the LORD; to retain and practice orderly worship focused on God's gifts; to keep one another in check as you zealously serve the LORD; for eyes to see and flee from sinful prejudice; to remember and celebrate God's deliverance; and for faith through suffering.

DAILY READINGS AND NOTES

MONDAY	TUESDAY	WEDNESDAY
Nehemiah 11–13	Esther 1–2	Esther 3–4

THURSDAY	FRIDAY	SATURDAY
Esther 5–7	Esther 8–10	Job 1

NEW INSIGHTS

FURTHER QUESTIONS

PERSONAL PRAYERS

HISTORICAL CONTEXT

Job was a righteous man of faith in the LORD from Uz, somewhere east of Canaan, perhaps more to the north. Job or one of his contemporaries likely wrote the book bearing his name somewhere in the broad range of 2200–1400 BC.

LAW AND GOSPEL THEMES

The overall theme of Job is that our right relationship with the LORD is purely the result of faith in His redeeming grace, but it also yields righteous living in response to that grace, even through suffering. Satan is a fallen angel who had no right to be in the presence of God but was permitted to be in the time of Job so key lessons might be taught. Satan is always under the control of the LORD. Job believed the LORD has the right to give or take from man as HE chooses. Eliphaz, Bildad, and Zophar wrongly based their rebukes of Job on their belief in the religion of man—that we get what we deserve based on what we do (see especially Job 8:2–6, 20). Job refused to give in to such false belief, holding to a higher view of God's goodness and justice.

WEEKLY MEMORY VERSE

Job 1:21, "The LORD gave, and the LORD has taken away; blessed be the name of the LORD."

LIFE APPLICATION STARTERS

How has or hasn't your faith led you closer to the LORD through your suffering? When have you slipped into the religion of man, thinking God acts only on YOUR worthiness of His love? How often have you heard someone say something like, "I HOPE I'm good enough to go to heaven"? How did you respond? How have you ascribed more power to Satan than is due to him?

PRAYER STARTERS

Pray for trust in the eternal goodness of God; for patience and faith, even through the trials of life; for faithful friends who will provide you with godly counsel when you need it; to not judge others based on the ills that befall them; and for the religion of God to prevail over the religion of man in our congregations, homes, and hearts.

DAILY READINGS AND NOTES

MONDAY	TUESDAY	WEDNESDAY
Job 2–3	Job 4–5	Job 6–7

THURSDAY	FRIDAY	SATURDAY
Job 8–10	Job 11–12	Job 13–14

NEW INSIGHTS

FURTHER QUESTIONS

PERSONAL PRAYERS

HISTORICAL CONTEXT

Job was a righteous man of faith in the LORD from Uz, somewhere east of Canaan, perhaps more to the north. Job or one of his contemporaries likely wrote the book bearing his name somewhere in the broad range of 2200–1400 BC.

LAW AND GOSPEL THEMES

It's easier to judge a sufferer with Law and argue theology than to bring the comfort of the Gospel (see Job 16:2). Job clung to God as his faithful witness (16:19) and Redeemer, expressing profound faith in a bodily resurrection (19:23–27). Even the faithful waver when suffering persists (see ch. 17). Job's friends proclaimed a "theology of glory"; that good people would have a good life. Job countered by saying that our only constant hope is in our unchangeable God (23:13). True, enduring wisdom and understanding come only from God through His Word of truth (28:28).

WEEKLY MEMORY VERSE

Job 19:25–26, "For I know that my Redeemer lives, and at the last He will stand upon the earth. And after my skin has been thus destroyed, yet in my flesh I shall see God."

LIFE APPLICATION STARTERS

Do you have friends like Job's who offer you poor counsel? Where else do you hear or see such poor counsel? Who will be your one sure advocate come Judgment Day? Why? Do you have a sure hope of rising from the dead with a perfect body? Why or why not? Have you seen the wicked prosper and the good suffer? How have you seen human reason and scientific knowledge fail to discern lasting truth? How does godly wisdom transcend what you see and reason for yourself?

PRAYER STARTERS

Pray to always seek and receive comfort from God's Word first, to be a friend who brings true comfort from God to the suffering, for eyes to look to Jesus as your constant friend and advocate, to trust in being declared right and raised with a perfect body come Judgment Day, and for true wisdom and understanding from God.

DAILY READINGS AND NOTES

MONDAY	TUESDAY	WEDNESDAY
Job 15–17	Job 18–19	Job 20–21

THURSDAY	FRIDAY	SATURDAY
Job 22–24	Job 25–28	Job 29–31

NEW INSIGHTS

FURTHER QUESTIONS

PERSONAL PRAYERS

HISTORICAL CONTEXT

Faithful Job lived in the land of Uz, east of Canaan. The Psalms are divided into five sections, or books, and were written by King David and various other authors between 1000–600 BC. They were used by Israel to learn and remember theological truths. Book One includes Psalms 1–41, intensely personal psalms written by David.

LAW AND GOSPEL THEMES

Elihu, being younger, waited for Job's three friends to finish speaking. He was angry with the three for not giving Job a godly answer and with Job for trying to justify himself. He wisely noted that no man should presume to tell God when and how to act. As Job 33:26 points out, God hears the prayer of the penitent and graciously grants righteousness. The LORD reminded Job that He alone is God, prompting Job's promise to stop justifying himself and humbly repent. The LORD graciously forgave Job and restored his fortunes. Psalm 1:6 carries on the theme of free grace as it says, "The LORD knows the way of the righteous." This is unconditional love, as a husband has for his wife.

WEEKLY MEMORY VERSE

Job 38:4, "Where were you when I laid the foundation of the earth? Tell Me, if you have understanding."

LIFE APPLICATION STARTERS

How can anger sometimes be fitting for a Christian when addressing sin? Who has the right to condemn sin? Why? Who is beyond the grace of God? Why does the LORD want us to humbly repent and turn to Him? When and how has the LORD blessed you in ways you know you did not deserve? Why did He? In a world filled with loneliness, what comfort is there in being known by the LORD? How can you share such love in your family and beyond?

PRAYER STARTERS

Pray to humble yourself before the LORD and do not seek to justify yourself; to rejoice that almighty God cares about you and wants to forgive you; for a truly penitent heart; for eyes to see God's many gifts; and to rejoice in being known by Jesus and to pass along this intimate and unconditional love to family, friends, and enemies.

DAILY READINGS AND NOTES

MONDAY	TUESDAY	WEDNESDAY
Job 32–34	Job 35–37	Job 38–41

THURSDAY	FRIDAY	SATURDAY
Job 42	Psalms 1–6	Psalms 7–11

NEW INSIGHTS

FURTHER QUESTIONS

PERSONAL PRAYERS

HISTORICAL CONTEXT

The Psalms are divided into five sections, or books, and were written by various authors between 1000–500 BC. Many of the psalms in this section were written by David, king of Israel, around 1000 BC. Book One includes Psalms 1–41, intensely personal psalms of David. Book Two spans Psalms 42–72, nationalistic psalms of David and his kingdom.

LAW AND GOSPEL THEMES

Lamentation, crying to the Lord for help, is fitting for the Christian, as it acknowledges that the Lord is our only hope. Many psalms express such faith (see especially 12–14). David beautifully foretold the resurrection of Jesus and believers to eternal life in the flesh (16:9–11). Our eternal hope gives us strength for today, as expressed in Psalms 17, 18, 21, 23, 27, 28, 31, and 46. David gave us powerful prophecies that were clearly fulfilled in the suffering, death, and resurrection of Jesus (e.g., Psalm 22), revealing God's timeless plan of salvation (25:6). Beautiful words from the Psalms bless us in the liturgy of the Divine Service still today (see 31:5 and the order of Compline in *Lutheran Service Book*, pp. 253–59).

WEEKLY MEMORY VERSE

Psalm 23:1, 3, 4, 6, "The Lord is my shepherd. . . . He leads me in paths of righteousness. . . . I will fear no evil. . . . I shall dwell in the house of the Lord forever."

LIFE APPLICATION STARTERS

The Psalms express the full range of thoughts and feelings that are part of our life in a sinful world: anger, sorrow, joy, hope, peace, and more. List all those you see as you read this week. What conviction and comfort do you receive as you relate to the perspective of the psalmists? Which psalm for this week is your favorite? Why? Listen for the psalms in the liturgy of the Divine Service and note their references when available, rejoicing that you are receiving God's gifts as the saints have done for three millennia. Our faith and practice are not transient human innovations. How is this unique and comforting?

PRAYER STARTERS

Pray to not be afraid to express your full range of thoughts to God in praying, confessing sin, rejoicing in grace, and overflowing in praise and that your worship will be guided by God's inspired Word and not human innovation.

DAILY READINGS AND NOTES

MONDAY	TUESDAY	WEDNESDAY
Psalms 12–17	Psalms 18–22	Psalms 23–28

THURSDAY	FRIDAY	SATURDAY
Psalms 29–34	Psalms 35–41	Psalms 42–47

NEW INSIGHTS

FURTHER QUESTIONS

PERSONAL PRAYERS

HISTORICAL CONTEXT

The Psalms are divided into five sections, or books, and were written by various authors between 1000–500 BC. Psalms 48–72, included in Book Two, were written by David from the kingdom period of David and Solomon at the time of the first temple. Psalms 73–82, part of Book Three, are nationalistic psalms from the time of Solomon in the tenth century BC and were mostly written by Asaph and the sons of Korah.

LAW AND GOSPEL THEMES

References to Zion and "the city of our God" should be taken as prophetic of Christ's kingdom and not exclusive to Jerusalem, since God allowed the temple and city to be destroyed as a result of Israel's sin. Christ's enduring kingdom, of which Christians are a part, will never fall. If we reject His reign in our lives, we will fall. Sinful from conception, we must trust only in Christ's mercy, which washes us in Baptism (Psalm 51) and makes God's "face to shine upon us" (Psalm 67). Trusting, we "shout for joy" (Psalm 66) and tell of the LORD's grace to the coming generations (Psalm 78).

WEEKLY MEMORY VERSE

Psalm 51:10–12, "Create in me a clean heart, O God, and renew a right spirit within me. Cast me not away from Your presence, and take not Your Holy Spirit from me. Restore to me the joy of Your salvation, and uphold me with a willing spirit."

LIFE APPLICATION STARTERS

What earthly city are you tempted to trust in? How can you always be a citizen in Christ's enduring kingdom? What does Psalm 51:5 teach about the origin of personhood and the depth of sin? How does that speak to your value to Jesus and your need for His grace to be saved? What are Christians obligated to give to the coming generations? How is this to be accomplished in the home? How can the Christian congregation be a partner in this?

PRAYER STARTERS

See page 845 of *TLSB* for a great way to use the Psalms in daily prayer. In *Lutheran Service Book*, each psalm verse is divided by an asterisk (*) and can be spoken responsively, making it perfect for interactive family prayer. Pray for the Lord to bless your personal and family prayer time using the Psalms. Ask the Spirit to work in the hearts of the next generations as you give them the Psalms.

DAILY READINGS AND NOTES

MONDAY	TUESDAY	WEDNESDAY
Psalms 48–53	Psalms 54–60	Psalms 61–66

THURSDAY	FRIDAY	SATURDAY
Psalms 67–72	Psalms 73–77	Psalms 78–82

NEW INSIGHTS

FURTHER QUESTIONS

PERSONAL PRAYERS

HISTORICAL CONTEXT

The Psalms are divided into five sections, or books, and were written by various authors between 1000–500 BC. Most of the psalms this week are anonymous and more difficult to date. Psalms 83–89 conclude Book Three. Book Four contains anonymous psalms and laments from Psalms 90–106. Psalms 107–150 make up Book Five, songs of ascents and praise written by David.

LAW AND GOSPEL THEMES

Psalm 86:15 says the Lord is "merciful and gracious, slow to anger and abounding in steadfast love." He does not give us the wrath our sins deserve but gives us gifts we do not deserve. Psalm 90, the only one attributed to Moses, speaks beautifully of the timeless love of God "in all generations. . . . From everlasting to everlasting" (vv. 1, 2). Our brief lives in the span of eternity are full of toil, yet the Lord uses us for His good purposes as He establishes "the work of our hands" (v. 17). Thus, we sing the words of the Venite (Psalm 95), "Oh come, let us sing to the LORD; let us make a joyful noise to the rock of our salvation!" (v. 1). Righteous anger is expressed in the Imprecatory Psalms such as 109, calling on the LORD for vindication.

WEEKLY MEMORY VERSE

Psalm 95:1, "Oh come, let us sing to the LORD; let us make a joyful noise to the rock of our salvation!"

LIFE APPLICATION STARTERS

The "steadfast love" of the LORD is another way of speaking about His undeserved, enduring, and abundant grace. Try to count all the times you see this phrase in this week's readings . . . if you can. The point the psalmists are making is that God's grace is beyond measure and is cause for all the praise. When anger or evil consumes you, call on the LORD for deliverance.

PRAYER STARTERS

Many verses in this week's psalms have been used by God's people in prayer throughout the past three millennia. Carry on that godly tradition, choosing some to use daily or weekly. For instance, a prayer commonly used at the end of meals is Psalm 106:1 (also 107:1 and 118:1). Try it yourself (or as a family) after every meal this week.

DAILY READINGS AND NOTES

MONDAY	TUESDAY	WEDNESDAY
Psalms 83–89	Psalms 90–95	Psalms 96–101
THURSDAY	**FRIDAY**	**SATURDAY**
Psalms 102–106	Psalms 107–113	Psalms 114–118

NEW INSIGHTS

FURTHER QUESTIONS

PERSONAL PRAYERS

HISTORICAL CONTEXT

The Psalms are divided into five sections, or books, and were written by various authors between 1000–500 BC. Several psalms this week are again ascribed to David, likely written around 1000 BC. Psalms 107–150 make up Book Five, songs of ascents and praise written by David.

LAW AND GOSPEL THEMES

Two psalms this week, 119 and 146, are acrostics, in which each new section or line has Hebrew words beginning with the successive letters of the Hebrew alphabet. This expresses the all-encompassing value of God's Word for life. An article on page 971 in *TLSB* speaks well to the power of God's Word in the writing of Psalm 119. Our response to God's Word should be one of praise, as expressed well in the final five psalms, known as Hallel Psalms, because they all begin and end with the phrase "Praise the LORD!" (in Hebrew, *Hallelujah!*).

WEEKLY MEMORY VERSE

Psalm 121:1–2, "I lift up my eyes to the hills. From where does my help come? My help comes from the LORD, who made heaven and earth."

LIFE APPLICATION STARTERS

Is there any gap in your life where God's Word is not currently finding application? Ponder how God's Word should apply there as well or even ask a church leader or fellow Christian to speak God's Word to you, thus completing the "acrostic" of your life. Do not doubt the steadfast love of Christ that covers ALL your life. Let that same friend who helped you apply God's Word also join you in praising Jesus for His steadfast love with a joyous "Hallelujah!"

PRAYER STARTERS

Write the alphabet down the side of a page. Write something you are thankful for that begins with each letter of the alphabet. Be sure to include Jesus and possibly some of His other titles or attributes, since He is the Alpha and Omega, or A to Z in English. Say a prayer praising the LORD for each item on your list, possibly as a responsive prayer with one person reading each word and the other family or group members responding with "Praise the LORD!" after each one.

DAILY READINGS AND NOTES

MONDAY	TUESDAY	WEDNESDAY
Psalm 119	Psalms 120–125	Psalms 126–134

THURSDAY	FRIDAY	SATURDAY
Psalms 135–137	Psalms 138–143	Psalms 144–150

NEW INSIGHTS

FURTHER QUESTIONS

PERSONAL PRAYERS

HISTORICAL CONTEXT

Most of Proverbs was written by King Solomon during his reign between 970–931 BC. Some sections were recorded by wise men in the time of King Hezekiah, between 715–686 BC.

LAW AND GOSPEL THEMES

Law and Gospel are clearly expressed in the theme of Proverbs, which is repeated throughout: "The fear of the Lord is the beginning of knowledge [GOSPEL]; fools despise wisdom and instruction [LAW]" (1:7). *Fear*, in this context, is a rich word that includes fright, awe, reverence, and trust (see *TLSB* p. 1001). The wicked are called to turn (1:23), or repent, that they might receive words of forgiveness and be made righteous. Trust, relying fully on God's grace, must replace sinful reason. Adultery is one of the most foolish ways of the wicked. Wisdom is associated with the Spirit and the preincarnate Christ (8:22; see also *TLSB* p. 1012). Arius (fourth century) wrongly understood 8:22 as saying Jesus was created and not eternal God.

WEEKLY MEMORY VERSE

Proverbs 1:7, "The fear of the Lord is the beginning of knowledge; fools despise wisdom and instruction."

LIFE APPLICATION STARTERS

How do you sometimes mistake human reason for the true wisdom of God that makes you righteous? Do you properly fear God in the full sense? How does your practice of Confession and Absolution impart wisdom? Why are the Spirit and Jesus necessary for wisdom? Why is adultery and all the sexual sins that go with it so utterly foolish?

PRAYER STARTERS

Pray that you will humbly receive God's Word of discipline, repent of trusting in your sinful reason, and receive the gifts of wisdom and righteousness by the work of the Holy Spirit and for Jesus' sake; for proper fear of the Lord, including genuine fear, awe, and trust; to see and flee the foolishness of adultery and all the evils that go with it; and in praise of your eternal, triune God.

DAILY READINGS AND NOTES

MONDAY	TUESDAY	WEDNESDAY
Proverbs 1–3	Proverbs 4	Proverbs 5–6

THURSDAY	FRIDAY	SATURDAY
Proverbs 7	Proverbs 8	Proverbs 9

NEW INSIGHTS

FURTHER QUESTIONS

PERSONAL PRAYERS

HISTORICAL CONTEXT

Most of Proverbs was written by King Solomon during his reign between 970–931 BC. Some were recorded by wise men in the time of King Hezekiah, between 715–686 BC.

LAW AND GOSPEL THEMES

This week highlights specific proverbs of Solomon found in 10:1–21:31. The first several chapters, up to 17:6, focus on what a father should teach his son. The rest warn against foolishness and give practical advice. "The way of the LORD is a stronghold to the blameless [Gospel], but destruction to evildoers [Law]" (10:29). Trust in riches is foolish. Hastily acquired wealth is quickly lost. The wise appreciate reproof and discipline. God is omnipresent and omniscient (15:3). God's judgment is more penetrating than our shallow and sinful self-evaluation (16:2). Silence is a virtue of the wise (18:2). A wise and prudent wife is a gift from the LORD.

WEEKLY MEMORY VERSE

Proverbs 14:12, "There is a way that seems right to a man, but its end is the way to death."

LIFE APPLICATION STARTERS

Martin Luther notes that Proverbs is a fitting handbook or prayerbook for daily usage by the righteous (see *TLSB* p. 996). How do God's words both condemn and comfort the wise? How do God's teachings about material riches contrast with the thoughts of foolish men? Why is it necessary to evaluate yourself according to the external Law of God and not just practice self-evaluation? What are the virtues of silence?

PRAYER STARTERS

The proverbs in this section are an excellent source of daily prayer. You could pray many of them by starting, "Lord, teach me that . . ." Pray for the conviction of these proverbs to drive you to the grace of Jesus, for strength to change your ways in line with these proverbs once you have been forgiven, and to value wisdom over wealth.

DAILY READINGS AND NOTES

MONDAY	TUESDAY	WEDNESDAY
Proverbs 10–11	Proverbs 12–13	Proverbs 14–15

THURSDAY	FRIDAY	SATURDAY
Proverbs 16–17	Proverbs 18–19	Proverbs 20–21

NEW INSIGHTS

FURTHER QUESTIONS

PERSONAL PRAYERS

HISTORICAL CONTEXT

Most of Proverbs was written by King Solomon during his reign between 970–931 BC. Some were recorded by wise men in the time of King Hezekiah, between 715–686 BC. Ecclesiastes was written by Solomon near the end of his reign, in approximately 931 BC.

LAW AND GOSPEL THEMES

The wise parent will train a child in godly wisdom (and penitent faith in Jesus) from infancy (see Proverbs 22:6; 23:13–14; 29:15, 17). Proverbs 23:11 speaks prophetically of Jesus, the Redeemer of orphans. Pure science is a wise endeavor as it discerns God's glory (see 25:2). Companions shape us, for good and bad, as iron sharpens iron (27:17). Chapter 31 beautifully describes a godly, wise woman. Ecclesiastes shows the end of a wise life marked by fear of God and obedience to His commandments. Fools who ignore this are destined to a life of vanity now and hell for eternity.

WEEKLY MEMORY VERSE

Proverbs 31:30, "Charm is deceitful, and beauty is vain, but a woman who fears the LORD is to be praised."

LIFE APPLICATION STARTERS

Children who learn godly wisdom have a great defense against Satan's temptation as they mature. How does a denial of God as Creator lead to foolish postulates and poor science? Why is fellowship with other Christians so important? What does Proverbs 31 teach Christian women? How does knowledge apart from the fear of God lead to despair (see Ecclesiastes 1:18)?

PRAYER STARTERS

Pray for parents who will discipline their children with godly wisdom and children who will cherish it; that the young will not abandon godly wisdom for sinful science and knowledge; for all Christians to cherish the blessing of fellowship with one another; for women to learn wisdom from God and His Word, such as is found in Proverbs 31; and that you will enjoy a meaningful life through humble fear of God and obedience to His Word.

DAILY READINGS AND NOTES

MONDAY	TUESDAY	WEDNESDAY
Proverbs 22–23	Proverbs 24–25	Proverbs 26–27
THURSDAY	**FRIDAY**	**SATURDAY**
Proverbs 28–29	Proverbs 30–31	Ecclesiastes 1–2

NEW INSIGHTS

FURTHER QUESTIONS

PERSONAL PRAYERS

HISTORICAL CONTEXT

King Solomon wrote Ecclesiastes near the end of his reign, in approximately 931 BC, and Song of Solomon near the beginning of his reign, around 970 BC.

LAW AND GOSPEL THEMES

Man's weak endeavors must yield to the immutable will of God; it is vanity to ignore this. Our work to save ourselves will fail. Serving our gracious God is our cause for joy. Two are better than one in marriage, church, and all of life, especially when Jesus is in the middle (Ecclesiastes 4:9–12; 9:9). Humble sorrow that leads to confession and faith in Jesus makes us truly glad (7:3). Kings and government are for our good in this life (7–8). Physical strength and accumulated riches are lost by time and chance (9:11). God alone controls our eternal spiritual destiny (12:7). Book knowledge must yield to godly wisdom (12:11–14). Proverbs and Ecclesiastes provide wisdom that leads to the joy of a bride as expressed in Song of Solomon. Israel, now the church, is the beloved Bride of Christ.

WEEKLY MEMORY VERSE

Ecclesiastes 12:13, "The end of the matter; all has been heard. Fear God and keep His commandments, for this is the whole duty of man."

LIFE APPLICATION STARTERS

How have you experienced the vanity of trying to find happiness apart from God? How can work, marriage, parenting, citizenship, and church life always be enjoyable even if they're not always fun? How can painful sorrow be a source of joy? How can sensuality in marriage direct us in faith to Jesus? How does sex outside of marriage hinder faith in Jesus?

PRAYER STARTERS

Pray to give up your vain pursuit of empty pleasures to the exclusion of joy in the Lord, for lasting joy in all earthly relationships as they follow God's wisdom, for godly scientists, for humble sorrow over sin that leads to the lasting joy of forgiveness for Jesus' sake, and that marriage will be cherished as an image of Jesus and His love for the church.

DAILY READINGS AND NOTES

MONDAY	TUESDAY	WEDNESDAY
Ecclesiastes 3–4	Ecclesiastes 5–6	Ecclesiastes 7–8

THURSDAY	FRIDAY	SATURDAY
Ecclesiastes 9–10	Ecclesiastes 11–12	Song of Solomon 1–3

NEW INSIGHTS

FURTHER QUESTIONS

PERSONAL PRAYERS

HISTORICAL CONTEXT

King Solomon wrote Song of Solomon near the beginning of his reign in approximately 970 BC. Contrary to critics' claims that three different authors wrote it, Isaiah, prophet and son of Amoz, wrote the entire book attributed to his name. He wrote from 740–681 BC but was prophesying future events through 480 BC (and even further, to Jesus and Judgment Day).

LAW AND GOSPEL THEMES

We often neglect the passionate love of our Bridegroom, Jesus, yet He never wavers in His devotion to us. He always delights in us and forgives our shallow love. Isaiah condemned the idolatry and rebellion of God's people, foretelling the Assyrian exile of Israel in 722 BC and the Babylonian exile of Judah in 587 BC. This week, note the "woe" phrases in Isaiah 5. Yet, starting primarily with chapter 40, he speaks comfort to the penitent exiles with clear prophecies of Jesus, the Suffering Servant. Isaiah's call in chapter 6 highlights the sinfulness of all men and the mercy and grace of Yahweh, who chooses us as His own and imparts His holiness to us as a gift.

WEEKLY MEMORY VERSE

Isaiah 1:18, "Come, . . . says the Lord: though your sins are like scarlet, they shall be as white as snow; though they are red like crimson, they shall become like wool."

LIFE APPLICATION STARTERS

Thank and encourage Christian couples who model the adoring love between Jesus and the church in their love for each other, especially those who have been committed for many years. Heed the words of God through Isaiah as clear warnings of pending judgment for idolatrous people of every age, including you. Rejoice in the comfort of prophecies fulfilled in Jesus and yet to see completion on Judgment Day and beyond.

PRAYER STARTERS

Pray in thanks for devoted and enduring marriages that reflect the love of Jesus and the church, in thanks for God's Word through faithful prophets like Isaiah, and for a humble heart to repent of your idolatry and receive comfort in Jesus.

DAILY READINGS AND NOTES

MONDAY	TUESDAY	WEDNESDAY
Song of Solomon 4–6	Song of Solomon 7–8	Isaiah 1–2

THURSDAY	FRIDAY	SATURDAY
Isaiah 3–4	Isaiah 5	Isaiah 6

NEW INSIGHTS

FURTHER QUESTIONS

PERSONAL PRAYERS

HISTORICAL CONTEXT

Contrary to critics' claims that three different authors wrote it, Isaiah, prophet and son of Amoz, wrote the entire book attributed to his name. He wrote from 740–681 BC but was prophesying future events through 480 BC (and even further, to Jesus and Judgment Day).

LAW AND GOSPEL THEMES

The overarching focus this week is on God's just judgment against sin . . . both that of the heathen nations (chapters 13–23) and of the whole world (chapters 24–27), including of His own people, Israel (chapter 22), as they reject Him. Yet, in the midst of His judgment, He gives glimpses of mercy, grace, and hope for restoration to those who repent and trust in Him. God's chastisement of King Ahaz brings us a clear prophecy of the birth of Jesus (7:10–14). Chapter 9 contains a beautiful description of Jesus as our Wonderful Counselor and more. The Trinity is at work for our salvation in 11:2. The LORD called Isaiah to bizarre behavior to speak His judgment and salvation by grace alone (see ch. 20). Death would be swallowed up forever by Jesus in His resurrection (25:7–8).

WEEKLY MEMORY VERSE

Isaiah 9:6, "For to us a child is born, to us a son is given; and the government shall be upon His shoulder, and His name shall be called Wonderful Counselor, Mighty God, Everlasting Father, Prince of Peace."

LIFE APPLICATION STARTERS

What power of man is able to stand against God and His wrath against sin? Are Christians safe from God's judgment? Is it true that once we are saved, we are always saved, no matter what we do? How does Isaiah, divinely inspired, clearly direct our eyes to Jesus as the one true Messiah? How is it that so many Jews do not see Jesus in Isaiah's words?

PRAYER STARTERS

Pray to humbly repent of sinful trust in your own power, that you will be spared from judgment against sin through faith in Jesus, that you listen to the Spirit and see Jesus as God's answer to your need for salvation, and for the strength to resist sin and stay in faith until Judgment Day and your deliverance.

DAILY READINGS AND NOTES

MONDAY	TUESDAY	WEDNESDAY
Isaiah 7–8	Isaiah 9–10	Isaiah 11–12

THURSDAY	FRIDAY	SATURDAY
Isaiah 13–20	Isaiah 21–23	Isaiah 24–25

NEW INSIGHTS

FURTHER QUESTIONS

PERSONAL PRAYERS

HISTORICAL CONTEXT

Contrary to the ideas of critics, Isaiah, prophet and son of Amoz, wrote the entire book attributed to his name. He wrote from 740–681 BC, prophesying future events through 480 BC (and even further, to Jesus and Judgment Day).

LAW AND GOSPEL THEMES

Isaiah 28–32 speaks of God's judgment on Samaria (the Northern Kingdom of Israel) and Jerusalem (the Southern Kingdom). Yet the promise of God's preservation of a faithful remnant is clear (see *TLSB* p. 1148). Hope lies in Jesus, the precious cornerstone (28:16). See *TLSB* page 1134 for a good treatment of God's wrath versus His persistent mercy and love. Chapters 33–35 are the central "hinge" of Isaiah, telling of disaster and hope. Chapters 36–39 relate Isaiah's interaction with King Hezekiah of Judah, who was blessed for his faithfulness but also foolishly opened the door to the later Babylonian exile.

WEEKLY MEMORY VERSE

Isaiah 35:3–4, "Strengthen the weak hands, and make firm the feeble knees. Say to those who have an anxious heart, 'Be strong; fear not! Behold, your God will come with vengeance, with the recompense of God. He will come and save you.'"

LIFE APPLICATION STARTERS

When have you foolishly trusted in human care and protection (as Israel turned to Egypt) only to be let down? What reliable source of strength and hope is described in detail in chapter 35? How does God's care for the "remnant" give comfort and hope to Christians today? How is Jesus your cornerstone? What great evil is expressed by Hezekiah in 39:8? How do parents fall into the same pitfall today, especially in spiritual matters?

PRAYER STARTERS

Pray that the Lord will lead you to sincere repentance and spare you from His judgment; to be numbered among the remnant of God's people who remain faithful to Him always; for complete trust in Jesus as your only sure foundation and cornerstone; to never become secure in your current state of peace; and that all parents will care for the spiritual well-being of the generations that follow, faithfully pointing them to Jesus.

DAILY READINGS AND NOTES

MONDAY	TUESDAY	WEDNESDAY
Isaiah 26–27	Isaiah 28–29	Isaiah 30–31
THURSDAY	**FRIDAY**	**SATURDAY**
Isaiah 32	Isaiah 33–35	Isaiah 36–39

NEW INSIGHTS

FURTHER QUESTIONS

PERSONAL PRAYERS

HISTORICAL CONTEXT

Contrary to the ideas of critics, Isaiah, prophet and son of Amoz, wrote the entire book attributed to his name. He wrote from 740–681 BC, prophesying future events through 480 BC (and even further, to Jesus and Judgment Day).

LAW AND GOSPEL THEMES

The chapters covered this week are some of the clearest declarations of Law and Gospel in all of Scripture. They declare comfort to God's chosen people, who humbled themselves and called upon Him for deliverance. This is beautiful typology as the words speak of deliverance from the Babylonian exile about two hundred years later; of salvation in the Suffering Servant, Jesus, about seven hundred years later (42:1–9; 49:1–13; 50:4–11; 52:13–53:12); and of the ultimate salvation of the faithful on Judgment Day, yet to come. Of course, salvation is only for the penitent remnant. The stubborn and impenitent masses will ultimately be condemned to hell on Judgment Day. Take note of the MANY prophecies in this section that are pointed out as they're fulfilled in the New Testament.

WEEKLY MEMORY VERSE

Isaiah 40:8, "The grass withers, the flower fades, but the word of our God will stand forever."

LIFE APPLICATION STARTERS

What comfort do you receive from the Word of the Lord through Isaiah this week? What warnings do you receive from Isaiah? Highlight all the references this week that clearly point to Jesus. How does such clear prophecy bolster your faith? How can you be the witness of this Good News to all people, as is so clearly called for by God (see Isaiah 42:6; 43:10; 44:8; 45:22; 49:1; 52:7)?

PRAYER STARTERS

Pray that you will humbly repent, receive salvation, and be comforted by God's promises that ARE fulfilled in Jesus and WILL BE more fully revealed on Judgment Day; for courage to be a witness of Law and Gospel to all people; and that the nations will repent and receive salvation with you.

DAILY READINGS AND NOTES

MONDAY	TUESDAY	WEDNESDAY
Isaiah 40–41	Isaiah 42–43	Isaiah 44–45

THURSDAY	FRIDAY	SATURDAY
Isaiah 46–47	Isaiah 48–49	Isaiah 50–52

NEW INSIGHTS

FURTHER QUESTIONS

PERSONAL PRAYERS

HISTORICAL CONTEXT

Isaiah wrote from 740–681 BC. The prophet Jeremiah, with his scribe Baruch, recorded God's Word, covering events beginning with Jeremiah's call in 628 BC and the reign of good King Josiah of Judah through Judah's fall in 587 BC and exile to Babylon.

LAW AND GOSPEL THEMES

As we conclude Isaiah, we see how the book is like a mini Bible—sixty-six chapters in Isaiah like the sixty-six books of the Bible, thirty-nine before Israel was saved and twenty-seven after the way of salvation had been revealed. Just as the New Testament still contains judgment against sin in the midst of the Good News of Jesus, so also these final chapters of Isaiah carry judgment against the proud sinner (66:24) amid rich words of grace to the penitent (see 53:5; 54:10; 61:1–3; 64:8; 65:17–25; 66:2). Chapter 53 vividly points to the Passion of Jesus. God's Word of judgment and salvation is sure and eternal (55:10–13). Chapters 56–66 make clear an Epiphany theme; salvation is also for Gentiles who repent. Jeremiah starts with his call to warn Judah of their pending exile in Babylon.

WEEKLY MEMORY VERSE

Isaiah 53:5, "But He was pierced for our transgressions; He was crushed for our iniquities; upon Him was the chastisement that brought us peace, and with His wounds we are healed."

LIFE APPLICATION STARTERS

Especially in chapters 61 and 62, Isaiah uses marriage imagery to clearly describe Jesus' love for us, His Bride. How does it affect you to know how much Jesus delights in you? Take note of the beautiful explanation in the article "A New Eden" in *TLSB*, identifying the "now and not yet" aspects of your salvation foretold by Isaiah. How does this give you hope today? YOU are to be a light to the Gentiles (see 60:1). GO and SHINE!

PRAYER STARTERS

Pray to see God's Spirit guiding all of Scripture to reveal His plan of salvation in Jesus; to flee God's wrath by humbly trusting in Jesus, your perfect Bridegroom; that you will rejoice in your marriage to Jesus and shine with the glow of a beloved bride; and for bold patience and hope now as you are sure of the new heaven and new earth that are not yet.

DAILY READINGS AND NOTES

MONDAY	TUESDAY	WEDNESDAY
Isaiah 53	Isaiah 54–57	Isaiah 58–59

THURSDAY	FRIDAY	SATURDAY
Isaiah 60–62	Isaiah 63–66	Jeremiah 1–2

NEW INSIGHTS

FURTHER QUESTIONS

PERSONAL PRAYERS

HISTORICAL CONTEXT

The prophet Jeremiah, with his scribe Baruch, recorded God's Word from 628 to approximately 580 BC, the period from good King Josiah of Judah through Judah's fall and exile to Babylon.

LAW AND GOSPEL THEMES

Jeremiah, though only a youth, was called to speak the Word of the LORD that had been put in his mouth (Jeremiah 1:9). This gave his word powerful authority to condemn sin (1:19). Marriage imagery is used to condemn Judah for rejecting the LORD, her Bridegroom (3:2, 20; 9:2). Yet the LORD is still willing to forgive the sincerely penitent (4:1–4). A true prophet, such as Jeremiah, grieves over the destruction of his people (4:19). False worship and sacrifice are condemned (7:21–26). We can only please God when we have genuine, humble faith in Him. Everything of your own making is worthless for salvation (9:23–24). Although God sometimes allows the wicked to prosper, He did not owe Jeremiah, nor does He owe you, an explanation for His ways, since He alone is God (chapter 12).

WEEKLY MEMORY VERSE

Jeremiah 9:23, "Let not the wise man boast in his wisdom, let not the mighty man boast in his might, let not the rich man boast in his riches."

LIFE APPLICATION STARTERS

Page 1220 in *TLSB* is a great summary of what constitutes faithful preaching from the prophets then and from preachers and teachers today. The focus is always on Jesus and salvation through Him alone. Who today is able to speak the Word of God with power? You? Can you and do you need to fully understand God's Word before you speak it? Are rot and drought today signs of God's coming judgment?

PRAYER STARTERS

Pray for boldness to speak God's Word of Law and Gospel, no matter your age or training; that Christian marriages will portray our loving relationship with the LORD; that all who hear and see you will know Jesus as Savior; and for faithful worship and sacrifice of yourself to the LORD.

DAILY READINGS AND NOTES

MONDAY	TUESDAY	WEDNESDAY
Jeremiah 3–4	Jeremiah 5–6	Jeremiah 7–8
THURSDAY	**FRIDAY**	**SATURDAY**
Jeremiah 9–10	Jeremiah 11–12	Jeremiah 13–14

NEW INSIGHTS

FURTHER QUESTIONS

PERSONAL PRAYERS

HISTORICAL CONTEXT

The prophet Jeremiah, with his scribe Baruch, recorded God's Word from 628 to approximately 580 BC, the period from good King Josiah of Judah through Judah's fall and exile to Babylon.

LAW AND GOSPEL THEMES

Jeremiah "consumed" God's Word as the source of true joy and delight (Jeremiah 15:16). When Jeremiah lamented over his accusers, the LORD assured him they would not prevail (15:20). Jeremiah was called by God to give up marriage, funerals, and feasting as a sign that such things will disappear in the coming judgment (ch. 16). God is the potter who has made you, so He has the right to destroy you. The LORD declared, "I swear by Myself," because there is no power greater than Him by which He might swear (22:5). See the charts of messianic prophecies on page 1245 of *TLSB*. You have God's Word to proclaim (23:28), which is better than sharing your dreams. False prophets like Hananiah lull people into complacency over sin by speaking of God's judgment as a minor "slap on the wrist" (ch. 28).

WEEKLY MEMORY VERSE

Jeremiah 15:16, "Your words were found, and I ate them, and Your words became to me a joy."

LIFE APPLICATION STARTERS

Do you consume God's Word like a delightful feast? How is it better than the most delicious meal? Why is Jeremiah's abstinence from marriage such a profound statement of judgment against Judah? Whereas false gods or prophets may swear "by heaven" or "all that is good," why is God swearing by Himself such a comforting Word of His power and care for you? How terrible will Judgment Day be for unbelievers?

PRAYER STARTERS

Pray to delight in God's Word as you daily consume it; that you will cherish the gifts of secure marriage and family life under the protection of the LORD; to courageously warn sinners of the terrible judgment of the LORD; and to joyfully share NOW Jesus as your Messiah and Savior from sin, death, and hell.

DAILY READINGS AND NOTES

MONDAY	TUESDAY	WEDNESDAY
Jeremiah 15–17	Jeremiah 18–19	Jeremiah 20–22

THURSDAY	FRIDAY	SATURDAY
Jeremiah 23	Jeremiah 24–25	Jeremiah 26–28

NEW INSIGHTS

FURTHER QUESTIONS

PERSONAL PRAYERS

HISTORICAL CONTEXT

The prophet Jeremiah, with his scribe Baruch, recorded God's Word from 628 to approximately 580 BC, the period from good King Josiah of Judah through Judah's fall and exile to Babylon.

LAW AND GOSPEL THEMES

This week's readings from Jeremiah jump back and forth in time, but all speak of God's discipline and restoration of Judah. Chapter 29 speaks hope to the exiles in Babylon, even though their exile would last seventy years. Chapters 30–33 are a "book of comfort" from Jeremiah to the exiles. Within these chapters are several messianic prophecies (see 30:22; 31:15, 31–34; and 33:11, 15, 18). Jeremiah 31:30–34 is a warning of judgment for sin but a comfort for those who are covered by the blood of Jesus. Each is responsible for his own sin. King Zedekiah feared the threats of men more than God and suffered a terrible end because of it. Jeremiah feared the LORD more than man and was spared because of it.

WEEKLY MEMORY VERSE

Jeremiah 31:34, "And no longer shall each one teach his neighbor and each his brother, saying, 'Know the LORD,' for they shall all know Me, from the least of them to the greatest, declares the LORD. For I will forgive their iniquity, and I will remember their sin no more."

LIFE APPLICATION STARTERS

When have you felt like God's discipline would never end, even though it was short in the span of eternity? How does Jeremiah's "book of comfort" still give you hope today? When and how have you been tempted to fear the threats of men more than trusting the promises of God? What comfort is there in knowing you will not be judged for anyone's sins but your own? Was Jeremiah a real man who actually suffered so much without losing faith? How could that be?

PRAYER STARTERS

Pray for perseverance when the LORD's discipline persists, to quickly return to the LORD in sincere penitence when His Word convicts you of guilt, and to trust in Jesus as the Messiah who HAS come and saved you and WILL come again and deliver you from the exile of sin.

DAILY READINGS AND NOTES

MONDAY	TUESDAY	WEDNESDAY
Jeremiah 29	Jeremiah 30–32	Jeremiah 33

THURSDAY	FRIDAY	SATURDAY
Jeremiah 34–35	Jeremiah 36–37	Jeremiah 38–40

NEW INSIGHTS

FURTHER QUESTIONS

PERSONAL PRAYERS

HISTORICAL CONTEXT

The prophet Jeremiah, with his scribe Baruch, recorded God's Word from 628 to approximately 580 BC, the period from good King Josiah of Judah through Judah's fall and exile to Babylon. Lamentations was written by Jeremiah after Judah's fall in 587 BC.

LAW AND GOSPEL THEMES

Rather than seeing their woes as a reason to repent and turn to the LORD, Judah followed their own reason and fled to Egypt for protection from Babylon, taking Jeremiah along. They even persisted in idolatrous worship of the "queen of heaven" (Jeremiah 44:17). Jeremiah condemned their evil and was likely martyred for it in Egypt. His scribe Baruch was preserved for remaining faithful while Judah was destroyed by Babylon, even in Egypt. Chapters 46–51 contain God's judgment against the Gentiles: Egypt, Philistine, Moab, Ammon, Edom (whose great wisdom failed them), Damascus, Kedar, Hazor, Elam, and mighty Babylon. "The LORD of hosts" (51:14) is above the universe. Judah lamented the result of her sin, her destruction, in 587 BC.

WEEKLY MEMORY VERSE

Jeremiah 51:5, "For Israel and Judah have not been forsaken by their God, the LORD of hosts."

LIFE APPLICATION STARTERS

When you're disciplined, do you ever dig your heels in and pursue sin all the more? What great nations have fallen? Will fall? What Kingdom alone will stand? Is it okay to lament over suffering? Where should it lead you? Will Jesus ever fail to hear and save you? How can this message help you connect with the world around you?

PRAYER STARTERS

Pray that you will not foolishly try to save yourself in your own way when you get into trouble, but that you will turn to the LORD and His ways alone; to boldly warn those who trust in themselves or any human power that they should trust only in the LORD; and for Jesus to hear your cries for help and deliver you.

DAILY READINGS AND NOTES

MONDAY	TUESDAY	WEDNESDAY
Jeremiah 41–43	Jeremiah 44–45	Jeremiah 46–49
THURSDAY	**FRIDAY**	**SATURDAY**
Jeremiah 50–51	Jeremiah 52	Lamentations 1

NEW INSIGHTS

FURTHER QUESTIONS

PERSONAL PRAYERS

HISTORICAL CONTEXT

Lamentations was written by Jeremiah after Judah's fall in 587 BC. Ezekiel was written by the prophet Ezekiel while he was already in exile from 593–570 BC, just before and after the fall and exile of Judah.

LAW AND GOSPEL THEMES

Jeremiah voiced the lament of Judah over their siege, pending destruction, and exile to Babylon. The acrostic pattern prevails, built on the twenty-two letters of the Hebrew alphabet. The heart of 3:22–24 is a triple Gospel light that will never be snuffed out at the center of this book of lament. The faithful priest Ezekiel, already in exile in Babylon (also known as Chaldea) in 593 BC, was called to speak God's Word along with bizarre actions. Ezekiel 1–24 contains judgments against Israel. Such harsh law is necessary to turn sinners from their way before they are condemned (see 3:19). God WANTS His people to be saved (6:8–14). A symbolic mark on the foreheads of the faithful in 9:4 (the Hebrew letter *tau*) would have looked like the Greek X, which is the first letter of Christ, foretelling our marking with the cross in Holy Baptism.

WEEKLY MEMORY VERSE

Lamentations 3:22–23, "The steadfast love of the LORD never ceases; His mercies never come to an end; they are new every morning; great is Your faithfulness."

LIFE APPLICATION STARTERS

God's Word and ways may still seem strange, but how does this fit with your true Holy God? How can you consume God's Word into your whole being? How are this week's readings consistent with the rest of Scripture? How are they unique? How do they speak to YOU? How have you been physically "marked for salvation"? Can this be lost?

PRAYER STARTERS

Pray that you properly lament over your sin and flee to the LORD in humble faith; that you consume the Word of the LORD and let it guide every part of your life; and for the courage and zeal to serve God faithfully, especially to warn stubborn sinners of judgment and then guide the penitent to salvation in Jesus alone.

DAILY READINGS AND NOTES

MONDAY	TUESDAY	WEDNESDAY
Lamentations 2–3	Lamentations 4–5	Ezekiel 1–2
THURSDAY	**FRIDAY**	**SATURDAY**
Ezekiel 3–5	Ezekiel 6–7	Ezekiel 8–9

NEW INSIGHTS

FURTHER QUESTIONS

PERSONAL PRAYERS

HISTORICAL CONTEXT

Ezekiel was written by the prophet Ezekiel while he was already in exile from 593–570 BC, just before and after the fall and exile of Judah.

LAW AND GOSPEL THEMES

The overall theme for this week is God's terrible, well-deserved judgment on rebellious Israel. God's glory left the earthly temple (chapter 10). Yet God would reign in the "new hearts" that received His Spirit (11:19–20). God's Word is sure (12:25). Chapter 16 uses coarse imagery to convey the utter adultery of the LORD's Bride, Israel, to awaken her to repentance. God's covenant promises endure (16:60). A sprig from a cedar clearly points to Jesus and hope for ALL people (17:22–24). Every individual is accountable to God for his or her own sin (18:4) and is able to receive personal grace (18:32). God's destruction of sinners is a threefold certainty, but His grace in Christ is still our sure hope (21:27). Read useful insights in "God's Throne" (p. 1323) and "Humor and Comedy in the Bible" (p. 1335) in *TLSB*.

WEEKLY MEMORY VERSE

Ezekiel 11:19–20, "I will remove the heart of stone from their flesh and give them a heart of flesh, . . . that they may walk in My statutes and keep My rules and obey them. And they shall be My people, and I will be their God."

LIFE APPLICATION STARTERS

How is your heart of stone replaced with a heart of flesh that is pleasing to God? How is 14:3 echoed in 1 Corinthians 1:23 and in your life? How does the LORD's love for His adulterous Bride give hope to even the most terrible of sinners? To YOU? How is individual accountability for sin both scary and comforting? How does an understanding of Law and Gospel help clarify all the imagery in Ezekiel?

PRAYER STARTERS

Pray that you learn from God's judgment against Israel, repent, and will be spared from the destruction they endured; to cherish the new birth of Baptism; to humbly stumble over your idolatry and turn your eyes up to Jesus to lift you; and that you lovingly condemn sinners but eagerly receive every single one who repents and receives Jesus.

DAILY READINGS AND NOTES

MONDAY	TUESDAY	WEDNESDAY
Ezekiel 10–11	Ezekiel 12–13	Ezekiel 14–15
THURSDAY	**FRIDAY**	**SATURDAY**
Ezekiel 16–17	Ezekiel 18–19	Ezekiel 20–21

NEW INSIGHTS

FURTHER QUESTIONS

PERSONAL PRAYERS

HISTORICAL CONTEXT

Ezekiel was written by the prophet Ezekiel while he was already in exile from 593–570 BC, just before and after the fall and exile of Judah.

LAW AND GOSPEL THEMES

Ezekiel suffered a terrible loss to make a point to Israel. His wife died, and he could NOT mourn over her, showing Israel they had no right to mourn over the loss of the temple. The LORD condemned seven evil nations around Israel (chs. 25–32). Though He used those nations to punish Israel, He still had to hold them guilty for sin. YET He would grant them mercy if they turned to Him (29:16). The fall of Egypt then persists to this day. Chapter 33 speaks of Ezekiel as a watchman for Israel, warning them. He must NOT fail to speak God's judgment, or he would face his own judgment because God has no pleasure in the death of the wicked (33:11). Verse 12 makes clear that we are not saved by our own righteous works but by grace alone. Jesus has become our one true Shepherd in fulfillment of 34:22–24.

WEEKLY MEMORY VERSE

Ezekiel 33:11, "Say to them, As I live, declares the Lord GOD, I have no pleasure in the death of the wicked, but that the wicked turn from his way and live."

LIFE APPLICATION STARTERS

How often do you mourn over losses that come as the result of your own sinfulness? What should cause your greatest mourning? How are you fulfilling your call to be a watchman to your family, your church, and your contacts in the world? Are you moved by vengeance or compassion when you speak God's Law? What comfort do you find in Jesus' lack of memory of your sin (33:16) and His care as your Good Shepherd?

PRAYER STARTERS

Pray that you do not mourn over lost idols but rejoice in God's gracious gifts, including His free forgiveness and eternal life; to boldly warn sinners of judgment out of love for them, seeking to share the Gospel; and in thanks to Jesus, your Shepherd!

DAILY READINGS AND NOTES

MONDAY	TUESDAY	WEDNESDAY
Ezekiel 22–23	Ezekiel 24	Ezekiel 25–27

THURSDAY	FRIDAY	SATURDAY
Ezekiel 28	Ezekiel 29–32	Ezekiel 33–34

NEW INSIGHTS

FURTHER QUESTIONS

PERSONAL PRAYERS

HISTORICAL CONTEXT

Ezekiel was written by the prophet Ezekiel while he was already in exile from 593–570 BC, just before and after the fall and exile of Judah.

LAW AND GOSPEL THEMES

Chapters 33–37 are a hopeful promise of new life for Israel, as the people would return from exile, and for us in the church, as we are set free from sin. Chapter 36 expresses this hope with strong baptismal imagery that has roots back to the beginning of creation (see p. 1369 of *TLSB*). Chapter 37 talks of new life using the imagery of dry bones that are raised to life by the speaking of God's Word and filling of the Spirit. Chapters 38 and 39 use the imagery of Gog (NOT meant to be one literal nation) to describe the wicked era in which we now live that will finally end when Jesus returns in judgment on the Last Day (see p. 1375). Chapters 40–48 speak of the peace, hope, and joy of worshiping the LORD in the new temple. This was partly fulfilled when Israel returned from exile, is more fully complete in US as the church, and will ultimately be fulfilled on Judgment Day when the Prince of Peace returns.

WEEKLY MEMORY VERSE

Ezekiel 36:25, "I will sprinkle clean water on you, and you shall be clean from all your uncleannesses, and from all your idols I will cleanse you."

LIFE APPLICATION STARTERS

Trace the acts of God from creation to deliver His people and bring new life "through water." How does this give greater understanding and value to your Baptism? How does Ezekiel comfort you in the face of evil enemies (Gog) and the death of the body (dry bones)? What does the detailed description of the new temple teach you about how you use your body, the temple of the Spirit, in worship today?

PRAYER STARTERS

Pray that you trust in God's control of all of history for your good, to be free from the fear of sin and evil, and to eagerly anticipate Jesus' victorious return on Judgment Day.

DAILY READINGS AND NOTES

MONDAY	TUESDAY	WEDNESDAY
Ezekiel 35–36	Ezekiel 37–39	Ezekiel 40–42
THURSDAY	**FRIDAY**	**SATURDAY**
Ezekiel 43	Ezekiel 44	Ezekiel 45–46

NEW INSIGHTS

FURTHER QUESTIONS

PERSONAL PRAYERS

HISTORICAL CONTEXT

Ezekiel was written by the prophet Ezekiel while he was already in exile from 593–570 BC, just before and after the fall and exile of Judah. Daniel was written by the prophet Daniel between approximately 605–536 BC. He was among the first exiles from Judea to Babylon.

LAW AND GOSPEL THEMES

In Ezekiel 47, water from the temple depicts the life-giving blessings of God's grace that still flow to us in Christ. Daniel rose to "rule" over Babylon and Persia with great wisdom after interpreting, by God's power, the dreams of Nebuchadnezzar (the tall man figure in chapter 2 and tree in chapter 4) and the writing seen by Darius in chapter 5. He was blessed by God for his faithful commitment to the Word, bringing comfort to the exiles and to us. His three friends were delivered from the fiery furnace (chapter 3), and he was delivered from the lions' den (chapter 6). He foretold the eternal kingdom of Jesus (2:44). Daniel called Nebuchadnezzar—and ALL people—to confession that absolution might be received for Jesus' sake (4:27).

WEEKLY MEMORY VERSE

Daniel 2:44, "The God of heaven will set up a kingdom that shall never be destroyed."

LIFE APPLICATION STARTERS

Is it okay for Christians to be honored and respected in worldly terms? What good can you do in this broken world? How does your citizenship in Jesus' kingdom give you hope? Where alone is true wisdom to be found? How are you being called to courageously stand up and speak the truth of God in this dying world? How will you be able to do it? Are we to be interpreting dreams today?

PRAYER STARTERS

Pray that you will go wherever God leads you to serve, even in earthly government; to be a witness to the LORD, no matter where you serve; that Jesus will be seen as Lord of all through you; for sincere repentance and faith in you and all to whom you witness; and for trust in Jesus' eternal reign.

DAILY READINGS AND NOTES

MONDAY	TUESDAY	WEDNESDAY
Ezekiel 47–48	Daniel 1	Daniel 2

THURSDAY	FRIDAY	SATURDAY
Daniel 3–4	Daniel 5	Daniel 6

NEW INSIGHTS

FURTHER QUESTIONS

PERSONAL PRAYERS

HISTORICAL CONTEXT

Daniel was written by the prophet Daniel between approximately 605–536 BC. He was among the first exiles from Judea to Babylon. Hosea was written by the prophet Hosea between approximately 740–715 BC during the time that the Northern Kingdom of Israel was conquered and taken into exile by Assyria.

LAW AND GOSPEL THEMES

The book of Daniel ends with his dreams and visions of what is to come for Judah and the Christian Church. Babylon would fall, and great powers, such as Alexander the Great of Greece, would arise. Still, Jesus would come to conquer Satan and will return to deliver His church at the end of time. These comforting promises are the main theme of Daniel that bring us hope and comfort even as we see the church under attack. Hosea is filled with rich marriage imagery to show God's "husband" love to us (2:16) and our constant rejection of Him, as we act more like a prostitute (1:2; 3:1) than a faithful wife. Hosea also has many clearly messianic prophecies (see 3:5; 6:2).

WEEKLY MEMORY VERSE

Daniel 12:2, "And many of those who sleep in the dust of the earth shall awake, some to everlasting life, and some to shame and everlasting contempt."

LIFE APPLICATION STARTERS

You should not try to interpret the dreams and visions of Daniel too specifically or try to determine the date of the end of the world. Still, how do our days fit the description of evil and persecution described in Daniel? What CLEAR words from Daniel give you hope and comfort (e.g., 7:13–14, 26–27; 12:1–3)? How are adulterous marriages a picture of the relationship between God and man? What does this say about the "Christian witness" power of a godly marriage?

PRAYER STARTERS

Pray that you do not fear the warfare, destruction, and persecution in your day but trust in Jesus as the ultimate victor; and pray for faithful, godly marriages that show Jesus to all, especially our children.

DAILY READINGS AND NOTES

MONDAY	TUESDAY	WEDNESDAY
Daniel 7–8	Daniel 9	Daniel 10–12
THURSDAY	**FRIDAY**	**SATURDAY**
Hosea 1–2	Hosea 3–4	Hosea 5–6

NEW INSIGHTS

FURTHER QUESTIONS

PERSONAL PRAYERS

HISTORICAL CONTEXT

Hosea was written by the prophet Hosea between approximately 740–715 BC during the time that the Northern Kingdom of Israel was conquered and taken into exile by Assyria. Joel was written by the prophet Joel likely between 848–800 BC, after the reign of pious king Jehoshaphat in Judah.

LAW AND GOSPEL THEMES

Hosea continued to warn Israel that her trust in men and idols would lead to her destruction. He recalled God's loving deliverance of Israel from Egypt in 1446 BC as he foretold deliverance from sin through Jesus, who would be called out of Egypt (11:1). Joel was likely one of the earliest prophets, warning all Israel of their destruction and exile. His talk of a locust attack may be an allegory (Assyria/Babylon) or literal. He didn't rage but lamented and pleaded. He foretold hope in the outpouring of the LORD's Spirit (2:28) and the gift of salvation given to all who call on the name of the LORD (2:32), as cited and fulfilled at Pentecost in Acts 2. Joel ends chapter 3 with a warning and promise concerning Judgment Day.

WEEKLY MEMORY VERSE

Hosea 2:16, "And in that day, declares the LORD, you will call Me 'My Husband.'"

LIFE APPLICATION STARTERS

How do you fear, love, and trust in idols rather than God? Where is your only hope for deliverance from your slavery to such sin? How do you see the Spirit of the LORD being poured out on people from all nations today? The Spirit leads us to humble penitence that calls on the name of the LORD for salvation. How is this visible in your worship practice regularly? Why is it necessary each week for your whole life?

PRAYER STARTERS

Pray that you never trust in men or the idols they create; that you humbly receive the Spirit in Word and Sacrament and freely confess your sin; and to be ready for your death and Judgment Day with a penitent, faithful heart.

DAILY READINGS AND NOTES

MONDAY	TUESDAY	WEDNESDAY
Hosea 7–8	Hosea 9–10	Hosea 11–12
THURSDAY	**FRIDAY**	**SATURDAY**
Hosea 13	Hosea 14	Joel 1

NEW INSIGHTS

FURTHER QUESTIONS

PERSONAL PRAYERS

HISTORICAL CONTEXT

Joel was written by the prophet Joel likely between 848–800 BC, after the reign of pious king Jehoshaphat in Judah. Amos was written by the prophet Amos between approximately 792–740 BC, shortly before Israel was conquered and exiled by Assyria.

LAW AND GOSPEL THEMES

Amos, whose name means "a burden," lived up to his name as he spoke a burdensome message of judgment from God, the roaring Lion (1:2), especially on the Northern Kingdom of Israel. He uses repeatedly in chapters 1 and 2 the phrase "for three transgressions and for four" to show their complete corruption. Almost all of his words are condemning, pointing out Israel's trust in wealth and human power along with their injustice and despising of the needy (5:24). Chapter 8 speaks a terrible threat from God as He warns of sending a famine on the land, a famine "of hearing the words of the LORD" (8:11). Only in the final verses of Amos (9:11–15) do we hear clear messianic hope of future restoration for Israel.

WEEKLY MEMORY VERSE

Joel 2:32, "And it shall come to pass that everyone who calls on the name of the LORD shall be saved."

LIFE APPLICATION STARTERS

Do people today (even you) ever act without fear of God's judgment on sin because their wealth and success lure them into thinking God approves of them? How would life be for you if you could never again hear the Word of God? How could you better appreciate the gift of God's Word? Do you or your church boldly uphold justice and righteousness?

PRAYER STARTERS

Pray to take seriously God's anger over sin and listen to the warnings of Amos and other prophets, that you will never become secure in your earthly wealth and safety, to cherish God's Word and never take it for granted, and that you will always promote and live by what is just and right.

DAILY READINGS AND NOTES

MONDAY	TUESDAY	WEDNESDAY
Joel 2	Joel 3	Amos 1–2
THURSDAY	**FRIDAY**	**SATURDAY**
Amos 3	Amos 4–5	Amos 6

NEW INSIGHTS

FURTHER QUESTIONS

PERSONAL PRAYERS

HISTORICAL CONTEXT

Amos was written by the prophet Amos between approximately 792–740 BC, shortly before Israel was conquered and exiled by Assyria. Obadiah was written by the prophet Obadiah in approximately 587–553 BC, in the time just after Jerusalem fell to the Babylonians. Jonah was written by the prophet Jonah in approximately 790 BC, before the fall of Israel.

LAW AND GOSPEL THEMES

Amos ended his warning against Israel with a brief word of messianic hope. Obadiah spoke the Lord's judgment on Edom, the descendants of Esau, for their evil treatment of Judah throughout history and especially at the fall of Jerusalem to Babylon. God was patient with them as He is with all people, but there is a limit, ultimately on Judgment Day (Obadiah 15 and 21). God is gracious and merciful to all who repent, even those whom you, like Jonah, may deem unworthy (Jonah 4:2). God even acted with mercy to Jonah by saving him in the belly of the fish. God's will never changes, but His loving way of dealing with you may change depending on your response (Jonah 3:10).

WEEKLY MEMORY VERSE

Jonah 4:2, "You are a gracious God and merciful, slow to anger and abounding in steadfast love, and relenting from disaster."

LIFE APPLICATION STARTERS

When and how have you become impatient with God's patience? Have you ever gone in a direction directly away from where God was leading you? How did that work out? Is there anyone you hope to NOT see in heaven? What does Jonah's story say about that? What could or should you do about that?

PRAYER STARTERS

Pray for obedience to the will of God in all of life; for courage to fulfill God's plans for you; in thanksgiving for God's patient love for you, even though you regularly run away from Him; to be patient with the persistent sinners in your life; that you show the mercy and grace of God to anyone, whenever possible; and for the salvation of ALL people, even those who seem to be too far gone.

DAILY READINGS AND NOTES

MONDAY	TUESDAY	WEDNESDAY
Amos 7	Amos 8	Amos 9
THURSDAY	**FRIDAY**	**SATURDAY**
Obadiah	Jonah 1–2	Jonah 3–4

NEW INSIGHTS

FURTHER QUESTIONS

PERSONAL PRAYERS

HISTORICAL CONTEXT

Micah was written by the prophet Micah likely between 750–686 BC, in the time when Israel was conquered and exiled by Assyria. Nahum was written by the prophet Nahum likely between 663–612 BC to comfort Israel, which was suffering under Assyrian power.

LAW AND GOSPEL THEMES

Micah was a contemporary of Isaiah and may have consulted with him, as many themes overlap (see Micah 4:1–3 and Isaiah 2:2–4). Micah indicted false shepherds over Israel who abused and misled them (see especially chapter 3). The book of Micah gives one of the most explicit rectilinear, or direct, prophecies (see *TLSB* p. 1493) of the coming of Jesus, stating He would be born in Bethlehem of Judea (5:2). Chapter 6 says those who are redeemed by the Lord will be led by the Spirit to do justice, love kindness (grace), and walk humbly (mercy) with God (6:8). Nahum portrays the Lord as a mighty warrior who fights for His chosen Israel and destroys her enemies, especially the oppressive Assyrian Empire and its capital of Nineveh. Though righteous in the days of Jonah, Nineveh had become utterly wicked.

WEEKLY MEMORY VERSE

Micah 5:2, "But you, O Bethlehem Ephrathah, . . . from you shall come forth for Me one who is to be ruler in Israel, whose coming forth is from of old, from ancient days."

LIFE APPLICATION STARTERS

All Christians, especially leaders in the church, are held to a high standard of showing justice, grace, and mercy. How successful is the church today in doing this, based on what you do and observe? What comfort do you receive from explicit prophecies such as Micah 5:2? What troubles or comforts you in Nahum's imagery of God as a mighty warrior? How do you balance your role as a humble servant with your role as a righteous warrior for the Lord?

PRAYER STARTERS

Pray that you will be able to stand for godly justice, share grace, and act with mercy in your dealings with all people; for the courage to defend the disenfranchised with the zeal of a warrior; and for all leaders of the church to live in the image of Christ.

DAILY READINGS AND NOTES

MONDAY	TUESDAY	WEDNESDAY
Micah 1–2	Micah 3–4	Micah 5

THURSDAY	FRIDAY	SATURDAY
Micah 6	Micah 7	Nahum 1–3

NEW INSIGHTS

FURTHER QUESTIONS

PERSONAL PRAYERS

HISTORICAL CONTEXT

The prophet Habakkuk wrote his book in approximately 605 BC, as Judah was threatened by Assyria but would fall to Babylon. The prophet Zephaniah wrote against Judah between 640–609 BC. The prophet Haggai wrote in a specific four-month period in 520 BC, as the people of Judah were to rebuild the temple. The prophet Zechariah was a contemporary of Haggai, writing from 520–518 BC.

LAW AND GOSPEL THEMES

Habakkuk lamented the LORD's slowness to deliver Israel from evil, for although Assyria could not overcome Judah, Babylon would. Yet he lived up to his name, meaning "embracer" (as one who hugs a child for comfort), as he spoke God's comfort (see especially Habakkuk 3:17–19). Like his contemporary Jeremiah, Zephaniah prophesied God's coming judgment on faithless and impenitent Judah, along with the surrounding nations. This warning (and hope for the faithful) is for all people of all time, as his lack of detail points clearly ahead to Jesus and Judgment Day. His closing song is vibrant with joy (3:14–20). Haggai chastised the people of Judah for taking care of themselves rather than rebuilding the temple after the Babylonian exile. He also gave hope from the Word of God. Zechariah spoke a similar message to Haggai.

WEEKLY MEMORY VERSE

Habakkuk 2:4, "The righteous shall live by his faith."

LIFE APPLICATION STARTERS

What comfort do you receive from Habakkuk's assertion from the LORD that "the righteous shall live by his faith" (2:4)? How does Zephaniah paint a vivid Law and Gospel picture of Judgment Day (for YOU too) in his three short chapters? What does Haggai teach you about your priorities?

PRAYER STARTERS

Pray to put your faith in Jesus as your highest priority and source of true life, to support the spread of the Gospel, and that you will be ready for Judgment Day through true repentance and steadfast faith in the Word.

DAILY READINGS AND NOTES

MONDAY	TUESDAY	WEDNESDAY
Habakkuk 1–2	Habakkuk 3	Zephaniah 1–2

THURSDAY	FRIDAY	SATURDAY
Zephaniah 3	Haggai 1–2	Zechariah 1–2

NEW INSIGHTS

FURTHER QUESTIONS

PERSONAL PRAYERS

HISTORICAL CONTEXT

The prophet Zechariah was a contemporary of Haggai, writing from 520–518 BC, the period during which the returned exiles of Judah obeyed God and began to rebuild the temple, which they completed in 516 BC.

LAW AND GOSPEL THEMES

Zechariah brought great comfort to the remnant in Judah as they were rebuilding the temple. His many interesting visions (four horns, a measuring line, a golden lampstand, a flying scroll, a woman in a basket, four chariots, etc.) primarily point to God's mighty power that will destroy evil and bring hope, especially at the coming of Jesus "in that day" (the New Testament era ending on Judgment Day). Joshua, the high priest, had his filthy garments replaced with pure ones as a type of how we, even Gentiles, passively receive absolution by grace through faith in Jesus (chapter 3). The Spirit (the Third Person of the Trinity) is needed for Zerubbabel and us to do God's will (4:6). Though they were rebuilding the temple, the true temple of the Lord is Jesus, our cornerstone, as foretold in the crown imagery of 6:9–15.

WEEKLY MEMORY VERSE

Zechariah 4:6, "Then He said to me, 'This is the word of the Lord to Zerubbabel: Not by might, nor by power, but by My Spirit, says the Lord of hosts.'"

LIFE APPLICATION STARTERS

How are we still building the temple of the Lord today? What opposition and challenges do we face, just as the Israelites did then? How is our practice of infant Baptism a beautiful fulfillment of the garment imagery in chapter 3? What role does the Holy Spirit continue to play in our work of building the Body of Christ, the temple of the Lord?

PRAYER STARTERS

Pray that you focus not on church buildings and programs but on Jesus, the temple of the Lord; to warn all sinners but also welcome them to Jesus' free grace and Holy Absolution as Judgment Day draws near; and that the Holy Spirit will fill and empower you for this work.

DAILY READINGS AND NOTES

MONDAY	TUESDAY	WEDNESDAY
Zechariah 3	Zechariah 4	Zechariah 5
THURSDAY	**FRIDAY**	**SATURDAY**
Zechariah 6	Zechariah 7	Zechariah 8

NEW INSIGHTS

FURTHER QUESTIONS

PERSONAL PRAYERS

HISTORICAL CONTEXT

Zechariah was written by the prophet Zechariah from 520–518 BC. Malachi was written by the prophet Malachi in approximately 430 BC, soon after the walls of Jerusalem had been restored.

LAW AND GOSPEL THEMES

Amidst his words of comfort for oppressed Israel, Zechariah offered several clear messianic prophecies: Jesus' Palm Sunday entry (9:9), Judas's betrayal (11:12–13), Jesus' crucifixion (12:10), Jesus and His disciples in Gethsemane (13:7). All show that Jesus is our ultimate source of comfort and hope. Malachi, which means "my messenger," was a priest and the final Old Testament prophet who faithfully spoke the LORD's call to repentance, especially for the priests who had not spoken truth or loved their wives as they should have (see 2:1–16). He foretold the coming of John the Baptist (3:1 and 4:5) to prepare the way for Jesus. He condemned the people for not giving proper tithes and offerings to God . . . so God could lovingly bless them even more abundantly (3:6–10).

WEEKLY MEMORY VERSE

Zechariah 9:9, "Rejoice greatly, O daughter of Zion! Shout aloud, O daughter of Jerusalem! Behold, your king is coming to you; righteous and having salvation is He, humble and mounted on a donkey, on a colt, the foal of a donkey."

LIFE APPLICATION STARTERS

What comfort and hope do the clear prophecies of Jesus this week give to you? What high calling is placed upon priests, pastors, and teachers of God's Word? What expectations are placed upon those served by these messengers? What do you learn from Malachi about proper stewardship and the tremendous blessings that go with it? What destruction is John the Baptist calling you to avoid, and how will you be spared?

PRAYER STARTERS

Pray that you see Jesus in all the Old Testament prophecies of the Messiah and receive His gift of salvation, to never turn from Jesus, to faithfully receive and share God's Word, and to be a wise steward who is truly blessed.

DAILY READINGS AND NOTES

MONDAY	TUESDAY	WEDNESDAY
Zechariah 9–10	Zechariah 11–12	Zechariah 13
THURSDAY	**FRIDAY**	**SATURDAY**
Zechariah 14	Malachi 1–2	Malachi 3–4

NEW INSIGHTS

FURTHER QUESTIONS

PERSONAL PRAYERS

HISTORICAL CONTEXT

Matthew, the apostle formerly known as Levi and a Jewish tax collector, wrote this Gospel account in approximately AD 50, around the same time as or slightly earlier than Mark and Luke.

LAW AND GOSPEL THEMES

Being a faithful Jew himself, Matthew wrote especially to a Jewish audience that would appreciate his many references to the fulfillment of Old Testament prophecy. Matthew's most important theme is the "kingdom of God" (heaven), which is mentioned forty-eight times by Jesus in this account. Matthew showed how the reign of King David found its fulfillment as Jesus came to establish God's reign on earth. This kingdom is visible now as penitent and forgiven believers share the love of Jesus they have received. The kingdom of God will be fully visible on Judgment Day when Jesus returns in power to claim His own and banish the unbelievers. The structure of Matthew is built around five "sermons": chapters 5–7, 10, 13, 18, and 24–25.

WEEKLY MEMORY VERSE

Matthew 1:22–23, "All this took place to fulfill what the Lord had spoken by the prophet: 'Behold, the virgin shall conceive and bear a son, and they shall call His name Immanuel.'"

LIFE APPLICATION STARTERS

How does it impact you to see Jesus so clearly revealed as the Messiah or Savior prophesied all through the Old Testament? What is the significance of the genealogy of Jesus in chapter 1, especially at this point in our Bible reading journey? Reflect on the significance of knowing you are a citizen of the eternal kingdom of God under the reign of Jesus. How is this especially helpful in our current geopolitical context?

PRAYER STARTERS

Pray that the Spirit will open your heart to recognize and trust in Jesus as the center of all of Scripture and ruler of the kingdom of God, in praise to God for your place in His eternal kingdom as a free gift of His grace for Jesus' sake, and to boldly proclaim the reign of Jesus to the world before He returns.

DAILY READINGS AND NOTES

MONDAY	TUESDAY	WEDNESDAY
Matthew 1–2	Matthew 3–4	Matthew 5–7
THURSDAY	**FRIDAY**	**SATURDAY**
Matthew 8–9	Matthew 10–11	Matthew 12–13

NEW INSIGHTS

FURTHER QUESTIONS

PERSONAL PRAYERS

HISTORICAL CONTEXT

Matthew, the apostle formerly known as Levi and a Jewish tax collector, wrote this Gospel account in approximately AD 50, around the same time as or slightly earlier than Mark and Luke.

LAW AND GOSPEL THEMES

In Matthew 16:19, Jesus gives "the keys of the kingdom of heaven" to His church. This is the power to forgive or retain sins. Chapter 18 highlights the usage of the keys by the church in the process of church discipline, which is to lead sinners to confession and forgiveness. In chapter 19, Jesus makes clear that marriage is the lifelong union of one man and one woman, just as it was established by God the Father at creation (see Genesis 2:24). Although Jesus was attacked by the Jewish leaders, He remained in control, teaching valuable lessons to His disciples then and now. Chapters 24–25 are rich with teachings from Jesus about the coming destruction of the temple, Judgment Day, and the eternal kingdom of God.

WEEKLY MEMORY VERSE

Matthew 19:6, "So they are no longer two but one flesh. What therefore God has joined together, let not man separate."

LIFE APPLICATION STARTERS

What comfort do you receive from proper usage of the "keys of the kingdom" in your life as part of the church? Why is proper church discipline a loving practice according to Matthew 18? Why are many Christian individuals and congregations hesitant to follow this practice? How do false practices today surrounding marriage destroy its blessing and its power as a Gospel witness? How are you to stand against those who attack you for your faith and witness?

PRAYER STARTERS

Pray to courageously care for others by calling them to repentance; that the Spirit will lead many to repent; for marriage to be preserved as a blessing to us and a Gospel witness to all; and for boldness in Jesus' name, even in the face of opposition.

DAILY READINGS AND NOTES

MONDAY	TUESDAY	WEDNESDAY
Matthew 14–15	Matthew 16–17	Matthew 18–19
THURSDAY	**FRIDAY**	**SATURDAY**
Matthew 20–21	Matthew 22–23	Matthew 24–25

NEW INSIGHTS

FURTHER QUESTIONS

PERSONAL PRAYERS

HISTORICAL CONTEXT

The apostle Matthew wrote his Gospel account in approximately AD 50. Mark, likely John Mark, the young disciple of Jesus who fled naked on the night Jesus was arrested in the Garden of Gethsemane, wrote his Gospel account from approximately AD 50–60.

LAW AND GOSPEL THEMES

In chapters 26–28, Matthew focuses on the suffering, death, and resurrection of Jesus as the sacrificial Lamb of God, who paid for your sin by the shedding of His blood. Jesus ended the need for the sacrificial system of the Old Testament. After His rising in victory, Jesus gave His disciples a clear purpose: to make disciples by baptizing and teaching in His name (Matthew 28:19–20). Mark is the shortest Gospel account, using simple, bold, expressive language to describe the dynamic, incarnate life of Jesus. He highlights the divinity of Jesus as the Son of God, using this title in 1:1 and throughout his account, specifically quoting this name from the mouth of the centurion who saw Jesus die a uniquely divine death on the cross (15:39). The two key parts of Mark are Jesus' public ministry (chapters 1–8) and His Passion (chapters 9–16).

WEEKLY MEMORY VERSE

Matthew 28:19–20, "Go therefore and make disciples of all nations, baptizing them in the name of the Father and of the Son and of the Holy Spirit, teaching them to observe all that I have commanded you. And behold, I am with you always, to the end of the age."

LIFE APPLICATION STARTERS

Who or what brings people to saving faith? How does this take the pressure off you in serving Jesus? What does this require of you in serving Jesus? Why might Mark be a good book of the Bible to be read by someone brand new to Christian teaching? How is Mark's Gospel account especially useful to parents and caregivers in discipling the next generations? What's the significance of Mark pointing out the divinity of Jesus?

PRAYER STARTERS

Pray in thanks to Jesus for being the sacrifice to end all sacrifices; in thanks to God for His work in Baptism and His Word to bring people to faith in Him and keep them there; that you faithfully point people to Jesus as true God, who could and did pay the price for our sin; and that more read and hear the Word of God and are brought to salvation.

DAILY READINGS AND NOTES

MONDAY	TUESDAY	WEDNESDAY
Matthew 26–27	Matthew 28	Mark 1–2

THURSDAY	FRIDAY	SATURDAY
Mark 3–4	Mark 5–6	Mark 7–8

NEW INSIGHTS

FURTHER QUESTIONS

PERSONAL PRAYERS

HISTORICAL CONTEXT

Mark, likely John Mark, the young disciple of Jesus who fled naked on the night Jesus was arrested in the Garden of Gethsemane, wrote his Gospel account from approximately AD 50–60.

LAW AND GOSPEL THEMES

Jesus was always in control of His life and ministry. Mark highlights the "Gospel secret" motif (see 4:11), reflecting that Jesus did not allow premature revelation of His true identity as the Son of God and Savior. For instance, see 9:9–10, just after His transfiguration. Jesus was not here to impress men or gain a huge following during His life but to defeat Satan and appease God's wrath against our sin. This may also explain the abrupt ending of his account at 16:8 (which many scholars believe is the original ending of Mark's account). Mark states what's important in 16:6, that "He has risen; He is not here." The victory was complete. We didn't NEED any more details. The powerful and true Gospel stands for eternity . . . for you and me. Mark's account of his naked escape (14:51) reveals that our call to serve is not based on our greatness but on the grace of Jesus.

WEEKLY MEMORY VERSE

Mark 10:45, "For even the Son of Man came not to be served but to serve, and to give His life as a ransom for many."

LIFE APPLICATION STARTERS

Why is it hard to serve a God who is not popular by human standards? What sustains you in serving such a God? Why is Jesus' bodily resurrection the most important teaching of our faith? How is this the focal point of all of Scripture? How have you been "caught naked" in your sins? What comfort do you receive in the inclusion of Mark's naked flight?

PRAYER STARTERS

Pray that you will not be concerned about your popularity among men when it comes to following Jesus, to rely fully on the Word and Supper of Jesus as your sustaining power for eternal life and service, in thanksgiving that Jesus lives in the flesh and you will too, and in praise for God's call of the weak and lowly.

DAILY READINGS AND NOTES

MONDAY	TUESDAY	WEDNESDAY
Mark 9	Mark 10	Mark 11

THURSDAY	FRIDAY	SATURDAY
Mark 12–13	Mark 14	Mark 15

NEW INSIGHTS

FURTHER QUESTIONS

PERSONAL PRAYERS

HISTORICAL CONTEXT

Mark wrote his Gospel account from approximately AD 50–60. Luke, the physician, was not one of the twelve apostles, but he knew them and traveled with Paul. He wrote his Gospel account from approximately AD 55–60.

LAW AND GOSPEL THEMES

The long ending of Mark may not have been written by him like the rest of his account, but its message is consistent with the rest of Scripture; it gives us the same mandate: to go to all and proclaim the Gospel, leading to Baptism and salvation by the work of the Holy Spirit. Luke, an educated physician, interviewed many witnesses and recorded an accurate account for Theophilus, who could have been a single person or symbolic of anyone who is a "friend of God" (the meaning of the name). He particularly wanted to share the message of Christ in a way that could be used for the catechesis (instruction) of those becoming and growing as disciples of Jesus (see Luke 1:4). Luke's account, therefore, is valuable for catechetical instruction in the home. Note his focus on the births and raising of John the Baptist and Jesus by godly parents.

WEEKLY MEMORY VERSES

Luke 1:37, "For nothing will be impossible with God."

Luke 2:14, "Glory to God in the highest, and on earth peace among those with whom He is pleased."

LIFE APPLICATION STARTERS

Even though it's not your job to make anyone believe (the Holy Spirit does that), how faithful are you in proclaiming the Gospel to the "whole creation"? Why did God use four different men to record the Gospel account? Is your home a place where catechesis is taking place using Luke's words? How could this be improved? How early in life should catechesis begin?

PRAYER STARTERS

Pray for courage and strength to proclaim the Gospel in all the world to the whole creation; to learn from all the words recorded about Jesus; to do your part to catechize others; and for every Christian home to be a primary place to teach the way of salvation in Jesus.

DAILY READINGS AND NOTES

MONDAY	TUESDAY	WEDNESDAY
Mark 16	Luke 1	Luke 2–3

THURSDAY	FRIDAY	SATURDAY
Luke 4–5	Luke 6	Luke 7–8

NEW INSIGHTS

FURTHER QUESTIONS

PERSONAL PRAYERS

HISTORICAL CONTEXT

Luke, the physician, was not one of the twelve apostles, but he knew them and traveled with Paul. He wrote his Gospel account from approximately AD 55–60.

LAW AND GOSPEL THEMES

Luke's focus on Christian catechesis (instruction) in the home reflects an emphasis throughout Scripture on such instruction happening in association with meals and feasts. Page 1718 in *TLSB* highlights many of these meals, such as Passover meals, wedding feasts (miracle at Cana), mass feedings by Jesus, and the Last Supper. God made us to be fed regularly in body and spirit. The Lord's Supper is a clear picture of this. Luke emphasizes that Jesus cared much for women, instructed them often, and relied on them for support in His ministry (see p. 1726 in *TLSB*). Jesus' resurrection is essential to our salvation and should be taught clearly (9:22). The Gospel "light" in us is needed in a dark world of sin (11:33–36). God WILL provide all we need in body and spirit (12:22–34). Along with home catechesis, weekly Sabbath (Sunday) worship, specifically receiving Jesus' Word and Supper, is essential.

WEEKLY MEMORY VERSE

Luke 15:7, "Just so, I tell you, there will be more joy in heaven over one sinner who repents than over ninety-nine righteous persons who need no repentance."

LIFE APPLICATION STARTERS

In addition to prayer, how can you help raise up more laborers for the Lord's harvest (see 10:2)? How should women be involved in receiving and sharing Christian catechesis? How are you a Gospel light to all the world? How can we use meals as a time for catechesis in the home, in the Christian congregation, and in the world? How does faithful, regular Sabbath worship reinforce Christian catechesis?

PRAYER STARTERS

Pray for the Lord to raise up more laborers to enter His harvest, using you to support this effort; for you to be able to shine the Gospel more clearly for all; to trust in God's desire to provide; and for faithful Sabbath worshipers.

DAILY READINGS AND NOTES

MONDAY	TUESDAY	WEDNESDAY
Luke 9	Luke 10	Luke 11–12
THURSDAY	**FRIDAY**	**SATURDAY**
Luke 13	Luke 14	Luke 15–16

NEW INSIGHTS

FURTHER QUESTIONS

PERSONAL PRAYERS

HISTORICAL CONTEXT

Luke, the physician, wrote his Gospel account from approximately AD 55–60. John, one of the twelve apostles and the only one not martyred, wrote his Gospel account in approximately AD 90.

LAW AND GOSPEL THEMES

Luke helps you better understand what happens to your body and soul when you die: the body decays after death, but your soul lives on with Jesus until it is united with your new, perfect body when it is raised on Judgment Day. See more on the body and soul in Luke 23:42–46, with Jesus' words to a thief and to His Father, in 16:19–31, and on *TLSB* page 1750. Whole households, even infants, can believe and be saved (18:15–17). To remember Jesus in His Supper is an act of faith in His power to save us (22:19). See *TLSB* page 1764 for helpful catechesis about Sunday, our "Sabbath," when we receive Jesus in Word and Sacrament. Right away in John 1:1–14, he responds to the heretic Cerinthus, who, in his day, denied Jesus' divinity. John highlights the divine and human natures of Jesus (note his many "I am" references). He also teaches deeper concepts about Jesus than any previous Gospel account as he shares many of Jesus' sayings and signs.

WEEKLY MEMORY VERSE

John 1:1, "In the beginning was the Word, and the Word was with God, and the Word was God."

LIFE APPLICATION STARTERS

What comfort do you have in Luke's teachings about life after death? What will you be like after Judgment Day? What does it mean to "remember" Jesus in the Lord's Supper? How can it be that Jesus is both fully God and fully man at the same time? Why is this truth important? How does John 1 beautifully tie together the Old and New Testaments? How does this support your faith?

PRAYER STARTERS

Pray that you do not fear death but anticipate eternal life in spirit and then body; to make every effort to lead entire families, including babies, to the gift of salvation in Christ; for faith in the power of Jesus' Supper; and to believe in Jesus as your fully God and man Savior from death and hell.

DAILY READINGS AND NOTES

MONDAY	TUESDAY	WEDNESDAY
Luke 17–18	Luke 19–20	Luke 21–22

THURSDAY	FRIDAY	SATURDAY
Luke 23–24	John 1–2	John 3

NEW INSIGHTS

FURTHER QUESTIONS

PERSONAL PRAYERS

HISTORICAL CONTEXT

John, one of the twelve apostles and the only one not martyred, wrote his Gospel account in approximately AD 90.

LAW AND GOSPEL THEMES

In addition to Jesus' teachings about His divinity, John recorded many profound truths about Jesus through His sayings and signs. Jesus provides you "living water" through His Gospel words (4:10). Jesus is your "bread of life" in His Word and Supper (6:35). In 8:58, Jesus uses the phrase only noted by John, "Truly, truly" ("Amen, Amen" in Greek), to teach the profound truth that He is timeless God, as He refers to Himself as "I am." Another "I am" statement by Jesus in 14:6 conveys the challenging "scandal of particularity" (see *TLSB* p. 1810). This is the hard and unique teaching that ONLY Jesus (NO other god or man) can save you from your sin. Yet it comforts us to know He gives certainty of salvation to ALL who receive Him. John also teaches that suffering is sometimes permitted by God for His higher, good purposes (9:3 and 11:15). The indwelling power of the Holy Spirit is a special focus of John, such as in 14:17 (see also *TLSB* p. 1815).

WEEKLY MEMORY VERSE

John 11:25, "I am the resurrection and the life."

LIFE APPLICATION STARTERS

Which of Jesus' profound statements in John are most challenging for you and why (see *TLSB* p. 1775, "Enigmatic Sayings"). Where alone do you hear pure, holy truth, and where are examples of it in John? Why is it important to know Jesus as "I am"? How is the "scandal of particularity" both scary and comforting? How can suffering ever be good?

PRAYER STARTERS

Pray to receive Jesus as your "living water" and "bread of life," that you and your household will believe and share the holy truth from John, that you will be able to guide sinners from doubt or anger to comfort in the teaching of Jesus as the only Savior, and for trust in God's goodness through your suffering.

DAILY READINGS AND NOTES

MONDAY	TUESDAY	WEDNESDAY
John 4	John 5–6	John 7–8

THURSDAY	FRIDAY	SATURDAY
John 9–10	John 11–12	John 13–14

NEW INSIGHTS

FURTHER QUESTIONS

PERSONAL PRAYERS

HISTORICAL CONTEXT

John, one of the twelve apostles, wrote his Gospel account in approximately AD 90. Acts was written by the physician Luke from approximately AD 60–62 as a continuation of the accurate historical account in the Gospel of Luke.

LAW AND GOSPEL THEMES

John records many miraculous signs performed by Jesus, especially in chapters 2–12, to reveal that He is the Messiah, fulfilling all the prophecies of the Old Testament. Yet, as noted in 20:30, His greatest sign was His resurrection from the dead, which proves His unique power to save all men from death and hell (note also 11:25). John conveys an important teaching about Jesus' kingdom, especially that it is not of this world (18:36–37). Confession and Absolution (the Office of the Keys), a powerful gift, was given by Jesus to the apostles and the church, as noted in 20:23. In Acts, Luke provides clear examples to illustrate the truth conveyed in his Gospel account—that all are justified by faith in Jesus alone and not by works of the Law. Both Peter and Paul led the way to proclaim this message in word and deed. Acts 1:8 describes this mission that began then and continues for us now . . . to all people!

WEEKLY MEMORY VERSE

Acts 1:8, "[Jesus said:] But you will receive power when the Holy Spirit has come upon you, and you will be My witnesses in Jerusalem and in all Judea and Samaria, and to the end of the earth."

LIFE APPLICATION STARTERS

Why is the resurrection of Jesus so important? What other signs performed by Jesus stand out to you and why? How is Jesus' kingdom different from all those of this world? Why is Confession and Absolution such a valuable gift? How are the Gospel of Luke and the book of Acts tied together? How is the miracle of Pentecost still impacting us? When and how have you received the Spirit's power for your part in Jesus' mission?

PRAYER STARTERS

Pray in thanks to Jesus for rising in victory from the dead to save you and give you Holy Absolution, in thankfulness that you are not required to earn your salvation, and for the Spirit's power to make you a bold witness of the Gospel as you faithfully go wherever He leads you.

DAILY READINGS AND NOTES

MONDAY	TUESDAY	WEDNESDAY
John 15–16	John 17	John 18–19
THURSDAY	**FRIDAY**	**SATURDAY**
John 20–21	Acts 1	Acts 2

NEW INSIGHTS

FURTHER QUESTIONS

PERSONAL PRAYERS

HISTORICAL CONTEXT

Acts was written by the physician Luke from approximately AD 60–62 as a continuation of the accurate historical account in the Gospel of Luke.

LAW AND GOSPEL THEMES

Luke makes clear in chapter 2 that Pentecost was focused on the clear proclamation of the Gospel of Jesus Christ to all the earth, not on us or any special powers we might possess. Peter showed this truth in action as he healed a lame beggar "in the name of Jesus Christ of Nazareth" (3:6) and taught of Jesus and not himself (3:12–16). Stephen was stoned to death as he remained a faithful martyr (Greek for "witness") for Jesus (see *TLSB* p. 1850 on martyrdom). The "grace and power" (6:8) of the Holy Spirit compelled Stephen with joy to the end. The zealous Jewish persecutor of Christians, Saul, was graciously and miraculously converted by Jesus and His Spirit to be the dynamic apostle Paul (chapter 9). Peter had a vision and divine appointments that made it clear the Gospel is for Jews and Gentiles (chapter 10).

WEEKLY MEMORY VERSE

Acts 10:28, "God has shown me that I should not call any person common or unclean."

LIFE APPLICATION STARTERS

What's the significance of Luke listing Jews from twelve geographic regions being present in Jerusalem to hear the Gospel in their own language on Pentecost? Are you a martyr for Jesus? Should you be? Who is unworthy to be a witness for Jesus and why? Which Gentile sinners are the most difficult for you to accept as worthy recipients of God's grace? Do you relate more with Peter or Paul? Why?

PRAYER STARTERS

Pray that the Holy Spirit will fill you with the grace and power to be a faithful witness for Jesus, even in the face of opposition or death itself; to accept all people as worthy recipients of God's mercy and grace; and for many to be moved to faith in Jesus by the Holy Spirit as they hear your witness.

DAILY READINGS AND NOTES

MONDAY	TUESDAY	WEDNESDAY
Acts 3–4	Acts 5	Acts 6–8
THURSDAY	**FRIDAY**	**SATURDAY**
Acts 9	Acts 10–11	Acts 12

NEW INSIGHTS

FURTHER QUESTIONS

PERSONAL PRAYERS

HISTORICAL CONTEXT

Acts was written by the physician Luke from approximately AD 60–62 as a continuation of the accurate historical account in the Gospel of Luke.

LAW AND GOSPEL THEMES

Paul boldly traveled along and near the northeast shore of the Mediterranean Sea on his three missionary journeys with various companions, including Luke. He made it explicitly clear that salvation was also for the Gentiles. The conversion of many Gentiles led to conflict, as many Jewish Christians insisted that these Gentiles must be circumcised in keeping with the law of Moses. A council of the believers in Jerusalem in AD 49 worked through the conflict in a wise and caring manner (see *TLSB* p. 1867), ending with the conclusion by James, based on Old Testament Scriptures, that the Gentiles are saved by grace and free from the restrictions of the Law. The only special requirement was that the Gentiles must act with respect for their Jewish brothers and sisters (chapter 15). Paul and Barnabas also acted in love to forgive each other after they had a conflict (Acts 15:39–41; 1 Corinthians 9:6).

WEEKLY MEMORY VERSE

Romans 3:23–24, "For all have sinned and fall short of the glory of God, and are justified by His grace as a gift, through the redemption that is in Christ Jesus."

LIFE APPLICATION STARTERS

What issues cause the greatest division among Christians today? What do you learn about reconciliation from the Jerusalem Council? How can you apply these lessons to the inevitable conflicts in your home with your closest family and friends? In what ways, then and now, does God turn setbacks to our mission endeavors into productive opportunities for witness?

PRAYER STARTERS

Pray that you are quick to confess your guilt in conflict and reconcile with others in the name of Jesus, for God's Word to always be your guide as you work through disputes with others, and for eyes to see and faith to follow where God is leading you as His witness.

DAILY READINGS AND NOTES

MONDAY	TUESDAY	WEDNESDAY
Acts 13–14	Acts 15:1–35	Acts 15:36–16:40
THURSDAY	**FRIDAY**	**SATURDAY**
Acts 17:1–18:23	Acts 18:24–21:16	Acts 21:17–23:35

NEW INSIGHTS

FURTHER QUESTIONS

PERSONAL PRAYERS

HISTORICAL CONTEXT

Acts was written by the physician Luke in approximately AD 60–62 as a continuation of the accurate historical account in the Gospel of Luke. Romans was written by the apostle Paul in AD 55 to the saints in Rome.

LAW AND GOSPEL THEMES

Paul was kept for several years (AD 55–68) in Roman custody in Caesarea and Rome. He used this time to continue his mission by proclaiming the Gospel in letters to the churches and audiences with Roman leaders. He illustrates our real-life practice of the Fourth Commandment as he obeyed the governing authorities while STILL putting God first in his life. Paul's letter to the saints in Rome is the Bible's clearest summary of the Gospel—in short, "The righteous shall live by faith." (1:17). All have sinned but are justified by God's grace as a gift for Jesus' sake (3:23–26). Still, only those who repent and receive the gift will be saved (5:1–2). Through the gift of Holy Baptism, we die to sin but rise to newness of life empowered by the Holy Spirit (6:1–4; see also *TLSB* p. 1920).

WEEKLY MEMORY VERSES

Romans 5:1, "Therefore, since we have been justified by faith, we have peace with God through our Lord Jesus Christ."

Romans 6:4, "We were buried therefore with Him by baptism into death, in order that, just as Christ was raised from the dead by the glory of the Father, we too might walk in newness of life."

LIFE APPLICATION STARTERS

Can you obey the government today and, at the same time, not compromise on your observance of any of God's Commandments? What opportunities are there for you to be a bold witness for Jesus WHILE living as a good citizen of your country? Try to speak the Gospel in fewer than ten words and explain what it means in fewer than two minutes. Whom has Jesus made righteous? Whom has Jesus saved from hell? How are you living out your Baptism?

PRAYER STARTERS

Pray for the wisdom to properly obey the government while not compromising on your obedience to God, to know the simple Gospel and speak it boldly and regularly, and to live out your Baptism daily.

DAILY READINGS AND NOTES

MONDAY	TUESDAY	WEDNESDAY
Acts 24–26	Acts 27–28	Romans 1–2
THURSDAY	**FRIDAY**	**SATURDAY**
Romans 3–4	Romans 5	Romans 6

NEW INSIGHTS

FURTHER QUESTIONS

PERSONAL PRAYERS

HISTORICAL CONTEXT

Romans was written by the apostle Paul in AD 55 to the saints in Rome as a clear summary of the Gospel of salvation through Jesus Christ alone.

LAW AND GOSPEL THEMES

Paul often draws on military imagery to illustrate the Gospel. Though evil will ever assail us in this world, we are utterly victorious conquerors through faith in Jesus (8:37). Saving faith is created and sustained in us by hearing the Word of Jesus recorded in Holy Scripture (10:17). Salvation is a gift to "all Israel" (11:26), which includes all who are children of Jacob through repentance and faith in Jesus (11:25–27), whether Jew or Gentile. Having been saved as a free gift from our merciful God, you are to "present your bodies as a living sacrifice," bearing witness to Jesus through incarnate love (12:1; see also *TLSB* p. 1934). Good Christians are also good citizens, humbly and daily subjecting ourselves to the governing authorities (13:1), even if we don't condone all their actions.

WEEKLY MEMORY VERSES

Romans 10:17, "So faith comes from hearing, and hearing through the word of Christ."

Romans 12:1, "Present your bodies as a living sacrifice, holy and acceptable to God, which is your spiritual worship."

LIFE APPLICATION STARTERS

In what sense are you already victorious over evil? Why is it so important to daily study and speak God's Word as it is recorded in the Bible? In what sense are you an Israelite? What, according to Paul, has replaced the animal sacrifices of the Old Testament (keeping in mind the actions of Jesus and now of every Christian)? Is sanctification an option or an obligation for us? Why? (See 15:1.)

PRAYER STARTERS

Pray that you live FROM your victory with Jesus, to be faithful in hearing and speaking the Word of Jesus, in thanks for being adopted into Israel, and to obediently and joyfully put your faith into actions of the flesh as a sacrifice to God.

DAILY READINGS AND NOTES

MONDAY	TUESDAY	WEDNESDAY
Romans 7	Romans 8	Romans 9–11
THURSDAY	**FRIDAY**	**SATURDAY**
Romans 12	Romans 13–14	Romans 15–16

NEW INSIGHTS

FURTHER QUESTIONS

PERSONAL PRAYERS

HISTORICAL CONTEXT

The book of 1 Corinthians was written by the apostle Paul in AD 55, before Pentecost.

LAW AND GOSPEL THEMES

Paul's primary focus in this letter was to condemn the division that had arisen among the Corinthian Christians as they had foolishly followed their own wisdom instead of that of Jesus Christ alone. It is faith in Jesus and the power of His love that would unite them again (1:10–13). God specifically chooses what is foolish in this world to show that it is only His power and wisdom that will save us (1:27). The crucifixion of Jesus is the prime example of God using what seems foolish to achieve His plan of salvation (2:2). God alone will build the church, not any man, including Paul (3:6–7). Man's sinful wisdom yields arrogance, unchastity (chapter 5), strife in the public courts (chapter 6), a lack of respect for godly marriage (chapter 7), and selfish trust in our knowledge (chapter 8). Like Paul, we humbly make ourselves servants to all for the sake of Christ and God's glory (9:19; 10:31).

WEEKLY MEMORY VERSES

1 Corinthians 1:27, "But God chose what is foolish in the world to shame the wise; God chose what is weak in the world to shame the strong."

1 Corinthians 2:2, "For I decided to know nothing among you except Jesus Christ and Him crucified."

LIFE APPLICATION STARTERS

When has following your selfish wisdom caused you to be divided from a fellow Christian? What division have you seen in the church due to bold trust in your own sinful wisdom and knowledge? Ask a trusted Christian friend to hold you accountable to not trust in your own ways but to humbly follow Jesus in all things. Whom do you need to forgive, love, and serve in humble obedience to Jesus?

PRAYER STARTERS

Pray that the divisions among Christians will be removed as you humbly confess your sins and call on your crucified Savior, Jesus, to forgive and unite us in His sacrificial love and to be a courageous fool for the Lord, reaching out in His power to save fellow sinners.

DAILY READINGS AND NOTES

MONDAY	TUESDAY	WEDNESDAY
1 Corinthians 1–2	1 Corinthians 3–4	1 Corinthians 5–6

THURSDAY	FRIDAY	SATURDAY
1 Corinthians 7	1 Corinthians 8–9	1 Corinthians 10

NEW INSIGHTS

FURTHER QUESTIONS

PERSONAL PRAYERS

HISTORICAL CONTEXT

The apostle Paul wrote 1 Corinthians in AD 55, before Pentecost, and 2 Corinthians before winter that same year.

LAW AND GOSPEL THEMES

The book of 1 Corinthians celebrates the gifts God gives for the good and unity of the church, especially love (chapter 13). Humble use of these gifts, particularly by the leaders of the church, will strengthen the church and glorify God (see *TLSB* p. 1969, "Speaking in Tongues"). Paul's direction for women to keep silent in the church (14:34) is intended to promote humble service in our God-given roles. God and Paul still value women and set them free, just like men, through the Gospel (15:1–10; see also *TLSB* p. 1972). Jesus' bodily resurrection, and ours, is central to our faith (chapter 15). The book of 2 Corinthians is primarily a letter of Gospel comfort to those cut to the heart by the Law (1:3–4). Paul tells us to forgive repentant sinners (2:7–8). He also points out that faithful ministers are still sinners ("jars of clay" in 4:7) who must point to Jesus alone as the source of power and comfort.

WEEKLY MEMORY VERSE

2 Corinthians 4:16, "Though our outer self is wasting away, our inner self is being renewed day by day."

LIFE APPLICATION STARTERS

How are you to prepare for the reception of the Lord's Supper per 1 Corinthians 11 (see also *TLSB* p. 1965)? Why is it important to hear Paul's teaching about women from the perspective of the Gospel, not Law? How do you do that? Even if you can't fully understand it, why is our bodily resurrection with Jesus so important and comforting? Where do you receive the power to comfort those who are afflicted under the Law of God? How are you a "jar of clay"?

PRAYER STARTERS

Pray to live in the true love of Jesus; that you will properly prepare to receive the Lord's Supper for your good; and for all Christians to humbly fulfill their vocations in a way that points to our crucified and risen Savior, Jesus, and comforts sinners.

DAILY READINGS AND NOTES

MONDAY	TUESDAY	WEDNESDAY
1 Corinthians 11–12	1 Corinthians 13–14	1 Corinthians 15
THURSDAY	**FRIDAY**	**SATURDAY**
1 Corinthians 16	2 Corinthians 1–2	2 Corinthians 3–4

NEW INSIGHTS

FURTHER QUESTIONS

PERSONAL PRAYERS

HISTORICAL CONTEXT

The apostle Paul wrote 2 Corinthians in AD 55 and Galatians from approximately AD 51–53.

LAW AND GOSPEL THEMES

In Christ, we are a new creation (2 Corinthians 5:17) and ambassadors for Him, imploring sinners to be reconciled with God (5:20). In any relationship, especially marriage, Christians are not to be unequally yoked with unbelievers (6:14). Rich in Christ, we are to share our treasures of body and soul with all (chapters 8–9). False apostles boast in themselves, but true apostles boast only in Christ and His gracious power (12:9). Paul ends 2 Corinthians with a powerful and instructive trinitarian blessing (13:14). As with the Corinthian Christians, Paul is galled by the Galatians having foolishly given up the Gospel truth for a lie (Galatians 1:6–9; 3:1). We can never justify ourselves by works of the Law (2:16). Paul even opposed Peter for leading others into such legalism by his hypocrisy (2:11–14; see also *TLSB* p. 2005 on legalism).

WEEKLY MEMORY VERSES

2 Corinthians 12:9, "But [the Lord] said to me, 'My grace is sufficient for you, for My power is made perfect in weakness.'"

Galatians 2:16, "Yet we know that a person is not justified by works of the law but through faith in Jesus Christ."

LIFE APPLICATION STARTERS

What "thorn in the flesh" have you endured that the Spirit has used to turn you to Jesus? What key advice does 2 Corinthians 6:14 give to those desiring to marry? Describe the comfort and power in Paul's blessing in 2 Corinthians 13:14. How does it sometimes seem easier to live by a set of laws (legalism) rather than to humbly trust in Jesus alone (Gospel)? What warning do you receive from Peter's fall into legalism and the need for Paul to rebuke him?

PRAYER STARTERS

Pray to rejoice that you are a new creation in Jesus, for courage to call sinners to be reconciled with God in Christ alone, for godly marriage between Christians, to never fall into legalism, and to humbly receive a loving rebuke and repent when you are rightly rebuked.

DAILY READINGS AND NOTES

MONDAY	TUESDAY	WEDNESDAY
2 Corinthians 5	2 Corinthians 6–7	2 Corinthians 8–9

THURSDAY	FRIDAY	SATURDAY
2 Corinthians 10–11	2 Corinthians 12–13	Galatians 1–2

NEW INSIGHTS

FURTHER QUESTIONS

PERSONAL PRAYERS

HISTORICAL CONTEXT

The apostle Paul wrote to the Galatians from approximately AD 51–53 and to the Ephesians in approximately AD 60.

LAW AND GOSPEL THEMES

As Paul warned the Galatians against the foolish sin of legalism (3:1), he still called them to live out their Gospel freedom with works of love, especially in chapters 5 and 6. When Paul says in 3:28 that there is "no male and female," he is speaking in the context of the Gospel. We are all equally forgiven by grace through faith in Jesus. This verse is not a directive for our daily vocations. Paul is not saying that males and females have the same roles of service to God and our fellow men. In our vocations, there are differences between men and women, parents and children, pastors and disciples . . . as we've heard throughout Scripture. Ephesians is filled with deep theological teaching, such as all that's packed into 1:3–14. Paul is especially clear on the distinction between grace and good works, justification and sanctification in chapter 2.

WEEKLY MEMORY VERSE

Ephesians 2:8–9, "For by grace you have been saved through faith. And this is not your own doing; it is the gift of God, not a result of works, so that no one may boast."

LIFE APPLICATION STARTERS

Having the assurance of free salvation by grace (justification), what works of love do you fail to fulfill (sanctification)? How is it dangerous to take verses of Scripture out of context, such as is often true for Galatians 3:28? What is Paul teaching with these words in Ephesians 1: *predestined*, *adoption*, *redemption*, *mystery*, *inheritance*, *hope*, and *guarantee*? Be prepared to use Ephesians 2:8–9 as the core of a clear Gospel witness . . . and NOW practice it with someone.

PRAYER STARTERS

Pray to rejoice in your assurance of salvation by grace through faith in Jesus, that you follow the assurance of salvation with bold works of love to God's glory, and to rightly understand the truths of Scripture from their context and then rightly apply them in your life and witness.

DAILY READINGS AND NOTES

MONDAY	TUESDAY	WEDNESDAY
Galatians 3	Galatians 4	Galatians 5–6

THURSDAY	FRIDAY	SATURDAY
Ephesians 1	Ephesians 2	Ephesians 3

NEW INSIGHTS

FURTHER QUESTIONS

PERSONAL PRAYERS

HISTORICAL CONTEXT

The apostle Paul wrote to both the Ephesians and the Philippians in approximately AD 60.

LAW AND GOSPEL THEMES

In Ephesians, especially chapter 4, Paul notes that all Christians are united as the one Body of Christ in Baptism and should be free from rivalry. We carry out our given vocations for the good of all in our new life together. This is clearly seen in lifelong marriage between one man and one woman, which is to be a living Gospel witness for the world to see the loving relationship between Jesus and His Bride, the church (5:31–32). Jesus' love also shapes the Christian home and all relationships (see 6:1–9 and *TLSB* p. 2025). Writing to the Christians in the Roman city of Philippi, Paul thanked them for their faith and loving mission support, also encouraging them to strain forward and live in a manner worthy of the Gospel they have received from Jesus (1:27). Our true citizenship, better than "Roman" or any other, is in heaven (3:20).

WEEKLY MEMORY VERSE

Ephesians 5:31–32, "'Therefore a man shall leave his father and mother and hold fast to his wife, and the two shall become one flesh.' This mystery is profound, and I am saying that it refers to Christ and the church."

LIFE APPLICATION STARTERS

Based on Ephesians 5:31–32, describe how the love Jesus has for you is sacrificial, unconditional, and incarnational. Explain how Christian marriage, and all relationships, are to be guided by such love as we live out a sanctified life. What armor does God give you for your life as a Christian in a sinful world (Ephesians 6:10–20)? How do you balance the Gospel of free salvation by grace with your duty to live in love and service all your days? How is Paul's call to be "straining forward" accurate for the challenge of living in faith and love your entire life?

PRAYER STARTERS

Pray in thanks to Jesus for loving you as your perfect Bridegroom; to reflect the love of Jesus in all your relationships; and that, being covered by God's armor, you will strain forward all your days in faith and loving service.

DAILY READINGS AND NOTES

MONDAY	TUESDAY	WEDNESDAY
Ephesians 4	Ephesians 5–6	Philippians 1
THURSDAY	**FRIDAY**	**SATURDAY**
Philippians 2	Philippians 3:1–4:1	Philippians 4:2–23

NEW INSIGHTS

FURTHER QUESTIONS

PERSONAL PRAYERS

HISTORICAL CONTEXT

The apostle Paul wrote to the Colossians in approximately AD 60 and to the Thessalonians (the first of two letters) in approximately AD 51.

LAW AND GOSPEL THEMES

Paul's letter to the Colossians is similar in outline and content to his letter to the Ephesians. He expresses deep theological concepts that celebrate our sure salvation, strength, power, joy, and eternal inheritance for Jesus' sake (1:3–23). He notes that suffering by Christians for the faith can bring life and hope to others (1:24). The key to Christian living is that we "do everything in the name of the Lord Jesus, giving thanks to God the Father through Him" (3:17). This is seen clearly in families marked by Christian submission, love, and obedience (3:18–25). Paul wrote his first letter to the truly faithful Thessalonian Christians to support them in his forced absence. He answered questions about life after death, bodily resurrection, and Jesus' return, not teaching the false idea of the "rapture" (4:13–5:11).

WEEKLY MEMORY VERSE

Philippians 1:21, "For to me to live is Christ, and to die is gain."

LIFE APPLICATION STARTERS

What treasures have you already inherited through your Baptism into Christ? Although Jesus is fully eternal God, in what sense is He "the firstborn of all creation" (Colossians 1:15–20)? What activities in your life are the most difficult for you to do in the name of Jesus? What will happen to your body and soul when you die? How does Paul refute the false teaching of the rapture of believers before Judgment Day?

PRAYER STARTERS

Pray that your sure salvation in Christ will fill you with strength, power, and joy even in suffering; to respond to the Gospel by doing everything in the name of Jesus; for Christian families to persevere in God's way even when under attack by Satan and the sinful world; and to trust that your soul is eternal and you WILL rise in the flesh on Judgment Day.

DAILY READINGS AND NOTES

MONDAY	TUESDAY	WEDNESDAY
Colossians 1	Colossians 2	Colossians 3–4
THURSDAY	**FRIDAY**	**SATURDAY**
1 Thessalonians 1	1 Thessalonians 2	1 Thessalonians 3

NEW INSIGHTS

FURTHER QUESTIONS

PERSONAL PRAYERS

HISTORICAL CONTEXT

The apostle Paul wrote 1 Thessalonians around AD 51 and 2 Thessalonians in approximately AD 52. He wrote his first letter to Timothy in AD 65.

LAW AND GOSPEL THEMES

In 2 Thessalonians, Paul picked up where he left off in his first letter to them by praising their faith. He encouraged patience in the face of suffering. He clarified his teaching in his first letter about the sudden return of Jesus, noting this had not yet happened and it was not imminent. Rome would fall and "the man of lawlessness" must be revealed before Jesus returns (2:3–4). They were to rebuke those who are idle because they think the end is at hand, a warning still valid for all Christians until Judgment Day. Paul wrote his first letter to Timothy, a young pastor and his "true child in the faith" (1 Timothy 1:2), as guidance for the early church, its pastors, and all its members. He gave specific guidance for the conduct of Christian women based on ethical (what's good in that context), theological (what's in accordance with God's good order), and missiological (what promotes Gospel witness) perspectives.

WEEKLY MEMORY VERSES

1 Thessalonians 4:13, "But we do not want you to be uninformed, brothers, about those who are asleep, that you may not grieve as others do who have no hope."

1 Timothy 2:5–6, "For there is one God, and there is one mediator between God and men, the man Christ Jesus, who gave Himself as a ransom for all."

LIFE APPLICATION STARTERS

Do you or other Christians today ever become tempted to stop serving and witnessing because Jesus is surely coming back at any moment? Where do you receive the strength to persevere in faith and service until Jesus returns? Practice articulating the way God (and Paul) values women while still calling them to unique vocations that are distinct from those of men.

PRAYER STARTERS

Pray that you will not be lazy or indifferent in living out your faith as you await Jesus' return, that all Christians will daily spur one another on to love and good works, and for good order in the church as we all fulfill our godly vocations.

DAILY READINGS AND NOTES

MONDAY	TUESDAY	WEDNESDAY
1 Thessalonians 4	1 Thessalonians 5	2 Thessalonians 1

THURSDAY	FRIDAY	SATURDAY
2 Thessalonians 2–3	1 Timothy 1	1 Timothy 2

NEW INSIGHTS

FURTHER QUESTIONS

PERSONAL PRAYERS

HISTORICAL CONTEXT

The apostle Paul wrote his first letter to Timothy in AD 65 and his second in AD 68 (his final known letter).

LAW AND GOSPEL THEMES

In his first letter to Timothy (and later in Titus), Paul explained key qualifications for pastors (referred to as overseers or elders). See the helpful chart on *TLSB* page 2080. He also warned against false teaching and guided Christians to proper conduct with contentment (6:6). In his second letter to Timothy, Paul encouraged him in the face of Roman persecution, which would soon lead to Paul's death as a martyr. Paul celebrated the power of God's Word (3:16–17) to make us righteous and to empower our good works. He commended Timothy's grandmother Lois and mother Eunice (1:5) for having instructed him in God's Word from childhood. That Word made him wise (often used as a synonym for faith) "for salvation through faith in Christ Jesus" (3:15).

WEEKLY MEMORY VERSE

2 Timothy 3:16–17, "All Scripture is breathed out by God and profitable for teaching, for reproof, for correction, and for training in righteousness, that the man of God may be complete, equipped for every good work."

LIFE APPLICATION STARTERS

As the qualifications for pastors are also good for all Christians, how well are you doing at living as God intends? How content are you in your godly life? How well would you stand up in the face of persecution, especially if threatened with death for your faith in Jesus? Summarize the power of God's Word as described in 2 Timothy 3:16–17. What role can faithful moms and grandmas play in the raising up of Christian children, even if no men are present in the home? Where can they find support for their task?

PRAYER STARTERS

Pray for faithful pastors and other church leaders who are qualified for service by the power of the Spirit; to avoid false teachers; for Christian contentment; and for all Christians to cherish God's Word and teach it in every home, to infants through adults and all generations to come.

DAILY READINGS AND NOTES

MONDAY	TUESDAY	WEDNESDAY
1 Timothy 3	1 Timothy 4	1 Timothy 5
THURSDAY	**FRIDAY**	**SATURDAY**
1 Timothy 6	2 Timothy 1	2 Timothy 2

NEW INSIGHTS

FURTHER QUESTIONS

PERSONAL PRAYERS

HISTORICAL CONTEXT

The apostle Paul wrote his second letter to Timothy in AD 68, his letter to Titus earlier in that same year, and his letter to Philemon in approximately AD 60. It is not clear who wrote the letter to the Hebrews, but it was sometime prior to AD 70.

LAW AND GOSPEL THEMES

In his letter to Titus, a pastor serving on the island of Crete, Paul directed him to condemn the gluttonous excess of the Cretans (1:12–13), especially their craving for false doctrines that appeal to our desire to please self. He directed modest and Christlike living for all—bishops (pastors), spouses, masters and servants, and Christians of all ages—that the Gospel would bless every part of life. That Gospel is beautifully stated in one long sentence in Titus 3:4–7. Paul's letter to a Christian master, Philemon, was an appeal for him to forgive and receive his runaway slave, Onesimus (meaning "useful"), who had been led to faith in Jesus by Paul. Paul acted like Jesus, who interceded with His heavenly Father to forgive and receive us since we are justified through faith in Jesus.

WEEKLY MEMORY VERSE

Titus 3:4–7, "But when the goodness and loving kindness of God our Savior appeared, He saved us, not because of works done by us in righteousness, but according to His own mercy, by the washing of regeneration and renewal of the Holy Spirit, whom He poured out on us richly through Jesus Christ our Savior, so that being justified by His grace we might become heirs according to the hope of eternal life."

LIFE APPLICATION STARTERS

Using the prompting of 2 Timothy 3:2–6, what selfish excesses tempt you to wander from your faith in Jesus like a Cretan? How do Paul's words in Titus 3:4–7 convey that you already have what matters "in excess"? Does your life reflect your gratitude for these gifts? How does the love of Jesus, received and shared, break down all social barriers, as shown in Paul's letter to Philemon?

PRAYER STARTERS

Pray for freedom from the selfish excesses of life that draw you away from all you have in Jesus, to live humbly with Christian love in whatever roles you fill, and to receive all fellow Christians as your equals.

DAILY READINGS AND NOTES

MONDAY	TUESDAY	WEDNESDAY
2 Timothy 3–4	Titus 1	Titus 2
THURSDAY	**FRIDAY**	**SATURDAY**
Titus 3	Philemon	Hebrews 1

NEW INSIGHTS

FURTHER QUESTIONS

PERSONAL PRAYERS

HISTORICAL CONTEXT

The letter to the Hebrews was written sometime prior to AD 70, when Jerusalem, including the temple, was destroyed by the Romans. The author is a well-educated Christian disciple, likely not Paul or one of the twelve apostles (see 2:3). Although Hebrews has difficult statements, it has been recognized by the church as being an authoritative part of the Bible since the second century.

LAW AND GOSPEL THEMES

First written most likely to a Jewish–Christian audience, Hebrews exults Jesus as the clearest revelation of God, above the Old Testament prophets (1:1–2). Jesus is also exalted as the greatest High Priest, who offered Himself as the perfect sacrifice to end all the sacrifices of the Old Testament system (7:27; 9:12). Jesus' blood now covers us in Holy Baptism, so we are fully justified before God. Our need for Jesus' sacrifice on our behalf is made clear by the Word of God (including the Old Testament), which is "living and active, . . . discerning the thoughts and intentions of the heart" (4:12).

WEEKLY MEMORY VERSE

Hebrews 4:12, "For the word of God is living and active, sharper than any two-edged sword, piercing to the division of soul and of spirit, of joints and of marrow, and discerning the thoughts and intentions of the heart."

LIFE APPLICATION STARTERS

In light of the Old Testament blood sacrifices that were required to pay for sin, what daily gratitude should you show to Jesus, the sacrifice to end all sacrifices? What richer imagery do you gain regarding Holy Baptism as it is tied to Jesus' sacrifice for you? Why is it valuable to study God's Word even when the truth sometimes hurts? What challenges will come your way when you faithfully speak God's Word, especially in your own home, as His witness to the world?

PRAYER STARTERS

Pray to show your thanks to Jesus daily for His perfect sacrifice on your behalf; to give thanks that Baptism covers your sins in the blood of Jesus, so you have risen with Him to eternal life; and to be a bold witness of God's Word always.

DAILY READINGS AND NOTES

MONDAY	TUESDAY	WEDNESDAY
Hebrew 2	Hebrews 3	Hebrews 4
THURSDAY	**FRIDAY**	**SATURDAY**
Hebrews 5	Hebrews 6	Hebrews 7

NEW INSIGHTS

FURTHER QUESTIONS

PERSONAL PRAYERS

HISTORICAL CONTEXT

The letter to the Hebrews was written prior to AD 70 by an anonymous but well-educated Christian disciple who had a thorough understanding of the Old Testament Scriptures but was likely not Paul or one of the twelve apostles.

LAW AND GOSPEL THEMES

Now that you are justified through the blood sacrifice of Jesus, our High Priest (10:12), you have a pure, "sanctified" conscience that's able to guide you to good works that honor God (9:14; 10:14). Once you know the truth of God's Word, you're to turn from sin by the power of the Holy Spirit. To continue sinning deliberately puts at risk your faith in Jesus and the benefit of His sacrifice for you (10:26–27). The faith of Old Testament martyrs and saints (as described in chapter 11) leads us to praise God, trust Him more, and imitate their faith. However, we have something those saints did not: "Jesus, the founder and perfecter of our faith," who not only justifies you but empowers you to run with endurance your race of faith (12:2). We know Jesus will not forsake us and man can not harm us, so you need not fear the power of men (13:5–6).

WEEKLY MEMORY VERSE

James 5:16, "Therefore, confess your sins to one another and pray for one another, that you may be healed."

LIFE APPLICATION STARTERS

Is there any sin in your life that you deliberately continue to practice even though you know you shouldn't? How does this "harden your conscience" and threaten your faith? Where should you turn first for help in this battle against sin? How can you empower fellow Christians, especially in your own home, to help you recognize and battle sin? Who alone will judge you for your sin? What comfort does that give you?

PRAYER STARTERS

Pray for wisdom and courage to recognize and sincerely confess the persistent sin in your life, to rejoice in the free forgiveness of Jesus and live in holiness out of thankfulness, and to be accountable to fellow Christians who are helping you turn from sin to sanctified living.

DAILY READINGS AND NOTES

MONDAY	TUESDAY	WEDNESDAY
Hebrews 8	Hebrews 9	Hebrews 10:1–18
THURSDAY	**FRIDAY**	**SATURDAY**
Hebrews 10:19–39	Hebrews 11	Hebrews 12

NEW INSIGHTS

FURTHER QUESTIONS

PERSONAL PRAYERS

HISTORICAL CONTEXT

The letter to the Hebrews was written prior to AD 70 by an anonymous but well-educated Christian disciple. James was most likely written by James, a half-brother of our Lord Jesus, in approximately AD 50 to Christian congregations dispersed among the Gentile nations beyond Jerusalem.

LAW AND GOSPEL THEMES

The book of James has many critics as it makes statements like "faith by itself, if it does not have works, is dead" (2:17). However, such teachings are fitting when they follow our justification by grace alone through the work of Jesus. James properly starts at this point as he says of our heavenly Father, "He brought us forth by the word of truth" (1:18). A Christian who HAS BEEN justified by Jesus SHOULD do good works that thank and honor Jesus in every part of life. See the articles on this topic on *TLSB* pages 2138–9. We should guard our tongues, be humble, avoid lust for wealth, be patient in suffering, and pray for one another. When you do fall, you must confess your sin and flee to Jesus for healing and strength to do good again (5:15–20).

WEEKLY MEMORY VERSE

1 Peter 3:21, "Baptism, . . . now saves you, . . . through the resurrection of Jesus Christ."

LIFE APPLICATION STARTERS

Is there any part of your life in which you are not fully living by faith and following Jesus' Word and ways? What impact will it have on your faith and certainty of salvation if you deny Jesus control of any part of your life? Which yields more truly good works in your life, the Law or the Gospel? What is "the prayer of faith" (5:15–16)? Does this match your typical prayers?

PRAYER STARTERS

Pray in sincere confession of the sin that infects any part of your life; in thanks for being declared righteous because of what Jesus HAS done for you; to faithfully live every part of your life in good works that honor Jesus; and to always pray FROM your faith in Jesus, your Savior.

DAILY READINGS AND NOTES

MONDAY	TUESDAY	WEDNESDAY
Hebrews 13	James 1	James 2

THURSDAY	FRIDAY	SATURDAY
James 3	James 4	James 5

NEW INSIGHTS

FURTHER QUESTIONS

PERSONAL PRAYERS

HISTORICAL CONTEXT

The apostle Simon Peter wrote 1 Peter to primarily Gentile Christians in Asia Minor, with Silvanus as his scribe and assistant, sometime before AD 67. Peter wrote 2 Peter to a similar audience in approximately AD 68, just before his death as a martyr.

LAW AND GOSPEL THEMES

In 1 Peter, the apostle is encouraging new Christians in Asia Minor to endure and grow in faith, even in the face of persecution for their righteousness. He points to the assurance of their salvation since they are baptized into Christ (3:21). He draws heavily on Old Testament imagery, such as Noah's deliverance through the ark, which corresponds to Holy Baptism and their holy election by God (2:9). He gives specific directions for Christian living in society and in the home, clearly guiding wives and husbands (3:1–7). Just before his execution, Peter warns in 2 Peter of false teachers who foster sinful living, thinking Jesus will not return to judge. We trust God's Word (1:21) to guide our faith and life until, at Jesus' return, we enter the new heavens and new earth (3:13).

WEEKLY MEMORY VERSE

2 Peter 3:13, "But according to His promise we are waiting for new heavens and a new earth in which righteousness dwells."

LIFE APPLICATION STARTERS

How is your situation as a Christian today similar to that of the new Gentile believers in Asia Minor who received Peter's two letters? How do Old Testament promises and your Baptism still strengthen your faith? What Gospel witness do wives and husbands, and ALL of us, give to the world when we follow Peter's guidance? Confident Jesus will come in judgment, what hope and compulsion do you have today?

PRAYER STARTERS

Pray for courage in the face of ridicule from a sinful world and misdirection from false teachers, to live in the sacrificial love of Jesus in all your relationships as a Gospel witness, and for joy and hope as you live assured of your place in the new heavens and new earth.

DAILY READINGS AND NOTES

MONDAY	TUESDAY	WEDNESDAY
1 Peter 1	1 Peter 2	1 Peter 3–4

THURSDAY	FRIDAY	SATURDAY
1 Peter 5	2 Peter 1–2	2 Peter 3

NEW INSIGHTS

FURTHER QUESTIONS

PERSONAL PRAYERS

HISTORICAL CONTEXT

The three epistles of John were written by the apostle John later in his life, between AD 85–95. He likely wrote from Ephesus, where he was an evangelist for about thirty years.

LAW AND GOSPEL THEMES

John's greatest focus is on the church as a family that is united in the love of Jesus. He begins 2 and 3 John by referring to himself as the "elder" and his recipients as beloved children. This references his role as a representative of Jesus to His church, made up of those called to be children of God (1 John 3:1) through faith. In deep love for the church, John calls us to true love (1 John 4:7–12), unlike the false, selfish teachers. He holds up Jesus as true God and man who alone paid the price (propitiation) for the sin of the "whole world" (1 John 2:2). The way of "light" is true love (1 John 2:9–11). As you abide in Jesus and His Word (1 John 4:13; 2 John 9), you'll never deny the Spirit and face damnation (see 1 John 5:16–18).

WEEKLY MEMORY VERSES

1 John 1:9–10, "If we confess our sins, He is faithful and just to forgive us our sins and to cleanse us from all unrighteousness. If we say we have not sinned, we make Him a liar, and His word is not in us."

1 John 4:7, "Beloved, let us love one another, for love is from God, and whoever loves has been born of God and knows God."

LIFE APPLICATION STARTERS

What does "elder" John teach about the role of a father in his home or a pastor in his congregation? How does a stable home where children abide in the unconditional love of Jesus teach them to be eternal children in the family of Jesus? How can a Christian congregation provide the same teaching for God's "children" of all ages? What sin has not been paid for by Jesus' crucifixion? Do you need to fear the sin that leads to death (see *TLSB* p. 2181)?

PRAYER STARTERS

Pray to respect and pray for your elders in your home and congregation who faithfully represent Jesus to the beloved children of God, that you are a faithful child of God who loves as He first loved you, that you never deny the Spirit and refuse to repent, and that you abide steadfast in Jesus' love in these end times.

DAILY READINGS AND NOTES

MONDAY	TUESDAY	WEDNESDAY
1 John 1	1 John 2:1–27	1 John 2:28–3:24
THURSDAY	**FRIDAY**	**SATURDAY**
1 John 4	1 John 5	2 John

NEW INSIGHTS

FURTHER QUESTIONS

PERSONAL PRAYERS

HISTORICAL CONTEXT

The book of 3 John was written by the apostle John later in his life, between AD 85–95. Jude was likely written by a half-brother of Jesus, not an apostle but an associate with them, in approximately AD 68. Revelation was written by the apostle John in either AD 68 (under the persecution of Nero) or AD 95 (near the end of his life). He likely wrote while he was in exile on the island of Patmos.

LAW AND GOSPEL THEMES

Jude was written to warn against false teachers. It cites nine references from the Old Testament (5–15) to warn of God's judgment against rebellion (see the chart in *TLSB*, p. 2189). Yet the author also encourages the faithful to rescue those entrapped in lies (23) and gives hope through a glorious doxological closing (24–25). John recorded his revelation from the Lord to celebrate the exalted reign of the Victor, Christ Jesus, and to comfort and encourage the church, the Bride of Christ, for her mission in these final days until Jesus returns in judgment (see *TLSB*, p. 2216). Jesus IS in control. Satan and evil will NOT prevail. The church WILL endure and spread to all nations until Jesus returns.

WEEKLY MEMORY VERSE

Jude 24–25, "Now to Him who is able to keep you from stumbling and to present you blameless before the presence of His glory with great joy, to the only God, our Savior, through Jesus Christ our Lord, be glory, majesty, dominion, and authority, before all time and now and forever. Amen."

LIFE APPLICATION STARTERS

What urgency is placed on you by God's consistent judgment on rebellion? How should you treat the ignorantly deceived as opposed to those who are blatantly rebellious against the truth of God's Word? How does it help to see Revelation as a book of images and figures for the comfort of Christians rather than as a timeline of world events? To what degree can Satan and evil assault us individually and as the church?

PRAYER STARTERS

Regularly pray Jude 24–25 as a source of comfort, power, and hope as you await Jesus' return in judgment. Pray for all to heed Christ's warning of judgment, repent, and be ready when He returns, and courageously tell of Jesus as Lord and Savior every day to all people before He returns in judgment.

DAILY READINGS AND NOTES

MONDAY	TUESDAY	WEDNESDAY
3 John	Jude	Revelation 1
THURSDAY	**FRIDAY**	**SATURDAY**
Revelation 2	Revelation 3	Revelation 4–5

NEW INSIGHTS

FURTHER QUESTIONS

PERSONAL PRAYERS

HISTORICAL CONTEXT

Revelation was written by the apostle John in either AD 68 (under the persecution of Nero) or AD 95 (near the end of his life). He likely wrote while he was in exile on the island of Patmos.

LAW AND GOSPEL THEMES

Chapters 4 and 5 are the heart of Revelation, focused on Jesus as the exalted and reigning LORD of the universe who will sustain and then save His Bride, the church. Revelation 5:9–10 is a good "capsule" picture of this theme. Jesus is the Lamb slain for the salvation of all who receive Him. The church is His kingdom in action on earth to bear witness to all. We have power over evil through Jesus. Chapters 6–21 are a series of visions of the end times and the coming day of judgment. Revelation 6:1–8:5 depicts Jesus opening the seven seals, a sign of His authority and deliverance of His Bride. Then, 8:6–11:19, with the blowing of seven trumpets, has a mission focus for John and the church.

WEEKLY MEMORY VERSE

Revelation 5:9–10, "Worthy are You to take the scroll and to open its seals, for You were slain, and by Your blood You ransomed people for God from every tribe and language and people and nation, and You have made them a kingdom and priests to our God, and they shall reign on the earth."

LIFE APPLICATION STARTERS

The shedding of blood to cover sin is a prominent theme throughout this entire Bible reading journey, pointing clearly to Jesus as the Lamb slain for us. How does Revelation 5:9–10 apply this theme to bring comfort and purpose to us who are in the church, the kingdom of God on earth? Knowing Jesus holds all the ultimate power of the universe, how does this impact your daily life in service to Him? As the Bride of Christ, what can all of us in the church learn from the example of a faithful Christian wife as she relates to her husband and children in God's way?

PRAYER STARTERS

Pray in thanks that you are covered by the blood of Jesus through Holy Baptism, Holy Absolution, and the Lord's Supper. Pray to be a faithful priest who boldly shares God's Word of judgment and deliverance.

DAILY READINGS AND NOTES

MONDAY	TUESDAY	WEDNESDAY
Revelation 6:1–8:5	Revelation 8:6–9:21	Revelation 10
THURSDAY	**FRIDAY**	**SATURDAY**
Revelation 11	Revelation 12	Revelation 13

NEW INSIGHTS

FURTHER QUESTIONS

PERSONAL PRAYERS

HISTORICAL CONTEXT

Revelation was written by the apostle John in either AD 68 (under the persecution of Nero) or AD 95 (near the end of his life). He likely wrote while he was in exile on the island of Patmos.

LAW AND GOSPEL THEMES

A third scene of the end times, depicted in Revelation 12:1–14:20, is a battle between the triune God and three evil opponents: a dragon, Satan (chapter 12); a first beast that embodies political power that opposes God (13:1–10); and a second beast that is a false prophet who seeks to destroy the church from within(13:11–18). While we don't take the number of the beast, 666, to be a literal mark on people or tie it to one specific human enemy of God, we do use God's perfect Word of truth to identify the complete imperfection of the lies of Satan that are evident in his servants on earth. Chapter 14 highlights the delivery, or harvest, of God's elect (144,000 is not literal but represents the completeness of 1212101010) by the Lamb, Jesus. Chapters 15 and 16 warn of God's wrath against evil. Chapters 17–19 foretell God's defeat of Babylon, the prostitute, and the coming celebration marriage feast for the Bride, the church.

WEEKLY MEMORY VERSE

Revelation 14:1, "Then I looked, and behold, on Mount Zion stood the Lamb, and with Him 144,000 who had His name and His Father's name written on their foreheads."

LIFE APPLICATION STARTERS

As part of the church who has been rescued by the great dragon slayer, Jesus, how does this comfort you in the face of Satan's attacks? What hope is yours in a political realm that is often opposed to the Christian Church? Stay in the Word of God daily so you can identify and destroy the lies of Satan and his servants. YOU are one of the 144,000 marked by the washing of Holy Baptism and filled with faith in Jesus. Jesus has a great marriage feast waiting for you on Judgment Day. Rejoice!

PRAYER STARTERS

Pray to stand firm amidst the dragon's flames, protected by Jesus' embrace, and that God's Word, read daily, will enable you to see and destroy Satan's lies in the world and the church.

DAILY READINGS AND NOTES

MONDAY	TUESDAY	WEDNESDAY
Revelation 14	Revelation 15	Revelation 16
THURSDAY	**FRIDAY**	**SATURDAY**
Revelation 17:1–18:8	Revelation 18:9–24	Revelation 19

NEW INSIGHTS

FURTHER QUESTIONS

PERSONAL PRAYERS

HISTORICAL CONTEXT

Revelation was written by the apostle John in either AD 68 (under the persecution of Nero) or AD 95 (near the end of his life). He likely wrote while he was in exile on the island of Patmos.

LAW AND GOSPEL THEMES

Revelation concludes with hopeful words of comfort for us who are in the church, the Bride of Christ. We are in the "thousand years" in which the church WILL continue as the kingdom of God on earth until Jesus returns as judge. Those raised to life through the means of grace have their names "written in the book of life" (20:15) and are reigning with the power of Jesus on earth. The fullness of this reign will come in the new heaven and new earth on Judgment Day, when the Bride of Christ will dwell with Jesus in the new Jerusalem (21:1–21) in glorious light forever (21:22–27). Anticipating this consummation of our joyous life with Jesus, we, His Bride, join the Spirit of God (22:17) in saying, "Amen. [YES!] Come, Lord Jesus!" (22:20).

WEEKLY MEMORY VERSES

Revelation 21:4, "[God] will wipe away every tear from their eyes, and death shall be no more, neither shall there be mourning, nor crying, nor pain anymore, for the former things have passed away."

Revelation 22:17, "The Spirit and the Bride say, 'Come.'"

LIFE APPLICATION STARTERS

What comfort is there in knowing Jesus is guiding history on His perfect timeline in this era of the church, His Bride, and that more Christians WILL continue to join us until He returns? In what sense have you already risen from the dead? Who or what can ever remove your name from the Lamb's Book of Life? Why should you be eager for Jesus to come in judgment? What should you be doing while you patiently await His coming? How do you envision the marriage feast that awaits you?

PRAYER STARTERS

Pray in joyous thanksgiving for all the riches you have received through this entire Bible reading journey and for comfort and strength through God's Word as you continue to study and meditate on it daily until your Bridegroom comes!

DAILY READINGS AND NOTES

MONDAY	TUESDAY	WEDNESDAY
Revelation 20	Revelation 21	Revelation 22

NEW INSIGHTS

FURTHER QUESTIONS

PERSONAL PRAYERS